T0048419

They Shoot Canoes, Don't They?

BOOKS BY PATRICK F. MCMANUS

Kid Camping from Aaaaiii! to Zip

A Fine and Pleasant Misery

They Shoot Canoes, Don't They?

Never Sniff a Gift Fish

The Grasshopper Trap

Rubber Legs and White Tail-Hairs

The Night the Bear Ate Goombaw

Whatchagot Stew
(with Patricia "The Troll" McManus Gass)

Real Ponies Don't Go Oink!

The Good Samaritan Strikes Again

How I Got This Way

Patrick F. McManus

THEY SHOOT CANOES, DON'T THEY?

A HOLT PAPERBACK

HENRY HOLT AND COMPANY   NEW YORK

Holt Paperbacks
Henry Holt and Company, LLC
Publishers since 1866
175 Fifth Avenue
New York, New York 10010
www.henryholt.com

A Holt Paperback® and 🔲® are registered trademarks
of Henry Holt and Company, LLC.

Library of Congress Cataloging-in-Publication Data
McManus, Patrick F.
They shoot canoes, don't they?
ISBN-13: 978-0-8050-0030-6
ISBN-10: 0-8050-0030-5
1. Outdoor recreation—Anecdotes, facetiae, satire, etc.
2. Camping—Anecdotes, facetiae, satire, etc.
3. Fishing—Anecdotes, facetiae, satire, etc.
4. Hunting—Anecdotes, facetiae, satire, etc.
I. Title.
GV191.6.M33   796.5'0207   80-24131

Henry Holt books are available for special promotions
and premiums. For details contact: Director, Special Markets.

Originally published in hardcover in 1981 by
Holt, Rinehart and Winston

First Holt Paperbacks Edition 1982

Designed by Joy Chu

Printed in the United States of America

D 71

All stories originally appeared in *Field & Stream* or
its allied publications, *Field & Stream Deer Hunting Annual* and
Field & Stream Fishing Annual, with the exception of "Meanwhile
Back at the B Western," which first appeared in *Colt American
Handgunning Annual 1979*, Aqua-Field Publications, Inc.

TO DARLENE

CONTENTS

Contents

They Shoot Canoes, Don't They?

All You Ever Wanted to Know About Live Bait but Were Afraid to Ask

☞ ☞ ☞ **S**urprisingly, many anglers are ashamed to admit that they fish with live bait. You'll run into one of these so-called purists on a trout stream and ask him what he's using. He'll say, "A Number thirty-two Royal Coachman on a three-ounce leader." Then he'll get a bite, snap his line out of the water, and there will be a worm on his hook. "That's the problem with these tiny flies," he'll say. "You keep catching worms with them."

The truth is that live-bait fishing has a long and noble history. Live bait was totally unknown to the early cavemen, who had to make do with a rather limited assortment of dry flies, nymphs, and a few streamers. One day, whether out of exasperation or simple impatience, a caveman made a backcast with a gray hackle he had not bothered to remove from a sage hen. Instantly, it was taken by a brontosaurus. The caveman was elated by his discovery, even though it was several centuries before anyone learned how to take a brontosaurus off the hook.

The caveman reasoned that if you can catch a

brontosaurus with live bait. you can surely catch fish with it, and he immediately began conducting experiments. He tried live chickens, ducks, and geese, but he soon found these very undependable, particularly on casts that passed directly overhead.

When he was about to give up and go back to dry flies, the caveman decided to bait his hook with a worm. He cast out into a deep, dark pool and immediately received the surprise of his life. A five-hundred-pound wild boar charged out of the brush and chased him for eighteen miles, and he never did learn whether worms were good bait.

Thus the discovery of worms as fishing bait was left to a humble cook in the army of Genghis Khan. After a busy day of conquering the Civilized World, the Khan decided he would like fish for supper and dropped a casual hint to one of his lieutenants. The lieutenant, who had had considerable experience with the Khan's casual hints, nearly trampled three foot soldiers getting the news into the kitchen. Dismounting, he said to the cooks, "Guess what? Old G.K. wants fish for supper." Since fishing had been extremely poor and no one had had so much as a nibble in days, the kitchen staff immediately bought tickets and caught the first stage out of town, the single exception being a little hors d'oeuvre specialist, Leroy Swartz, who knew absolutely nothing about fishing. Leroy had never developed the knack for plundering and pillaging—though he wasn't bad at razing—and as a result his total loot for the campaign was a spade with a broken handle. For a reason known only to Leroy, he started digging up the ground with the spade. The lieutenant, assuming he was digging a grave, said, "If we can't get G.K. any fish for his supper, you might as well make that big enough for two." Then Leroy started picking up worms and stuffing them into his pocket, tomato cans not yet having been invented. He grabbed a fishing pole and went off to the nearest river, from whence he shortly returned with his limit, in those days as many as you could carry plus one fish. Everyone danced and shouted over Leroy's discovery that worms were excellent fishing bait. Even the Khan was beside himself with joy, a condition that caused Mrs. Khan considerable annoyance since they slept in the same bed. Leroy Swartz was henceforth known as the Father of Worms, a title he did not much care for, but it beat employment as a battering ram on the next fortress to be attacked.

Toward the latter part of the eighteenth century, grasshoppers were discovered to be exceptional live bait. Up until then they were thought to be good only for devouring grain crops and causing widespread famine. One day an angler was walking along a country road in search of a good place to dig a supply of worms. He happened to glance out into a field fairly alive with grasshoppers and noticed a man leaping about on all fours and slapping the ground with his hat. The angler thought the fellow must be crazy to behave in such a strange manner and walked over to see what he was up to. It turned out the man *was* crazy, but the angler didn't discover this until he had helped him catch a dozen grasshoppers. Since by then it was too late to dig any worms, the angler decided to bait his hook with grasshoppers—and the rest is history.

Up until the Industrial Revolution and the invention of tomato cans and the flat tobacco can, there were no suitable containers for live bait, and anglers had to carry their bait around in their hands, pockets, and hats. In the case of grasshoppers, wealthy fishermen would sometimes hire a boy to drive a herd of them along the bank. In later years worms were carried in pokes similar to those used for gold coins. There is at least one recorded instance in which a card-playing fisherman narrowly escaped lynching when he attempted to bluff with a poke of nightcrawlers.

So much for the history of live bait. We will now examine some of the various kinds of live bait, where to find it, how to preserve it, and assorted techniques for using it.

First off, there are only two kinds of bait: live bait and dead bait. Worms, grubs, grasshoppers, minnows, and the like are live bait, unless left unattended in a hot car too long, in which case they become dead bait. I have on occasion forgotten to remove a can of worms from my car on a blistering July day, a mistake that has led to attempts to bait hooks with little balls of worm paste, not to mention the necessity of driving with all the car's windows open until approximately the middle of February. On the other hand, I've carried around salmon eggs and pickled pork rind until they were showing definite signs of life.

My favorite method of preserving live bait is to store it in the refrigerator until it is ready for use. There are two schools of thought on the proper execution of this procedure. Some hold it is better to tell your wife first, and the others claim it is better to let her make the discovery for herself. I'm a member of the latter group and have been ever since my wife came across a jar of my hellgrammites while she was sorting through the refrigerator in search of some mayonnaise. The incident would probably have passed without any lingering ill effects had she not at the time been entertaining her church bridge club. It is difficult to describe the resulting commotion with any accuracy, but I learned later that cards from our bridge deck were found as far away as three blocks and one of the olive-and-avocado sandwiches served at the party turned up in a ladies' restroom halfway across town. Our dog was asleep on the front sidewalk when the ladies left, and it was weeks before we could get all the dents out of him left by their heels.

I have on occasion attempted to lay in a supply of worms during the spring months while they are still near the surface and one doesn't have to dig down to the aquifer to find them. I'll stash a couple of hundred of them in a washtub filled with dirt and feed them coffee grounds. The reason I feed them coffee grounds is that numerous people have told me that that is what worms like to eat. Whether they do or not, I'm not sure. In any case, I've yet to find a single worm when I dump out the tub later in the summer. I'm beginning to suspect that worms can't stand coffee grounds (or maybe coffee grounds like worms). When you stop to think about it, where would your average worm develop a taste for coffee anyway?

The beginning angler is often of the impression that there are only three kinds of worms: small, medium, and large. Actually, the size of the worm makes little difference. Temperament and character are everything. These two characteristics seem to be determined primarily by environment. For example, I've never found a worm raised in a manure pile who could earn his keep as fishing bait. Manure-pile worms are soft and pale and accustomed to easy living. To a worm, a manure pile is a suite in the Ritz, a villa on the Riviera. He never has to worry about where his next meal is coming from. (If he knew, he would probably worry, but he doesn't know.) Manure-pile worms don't have any street savvy. Now, you dig up a worm out of a garden, an individual who has been through a couple of rototillings, and that worm has been around. He's going to go out and put up a good fight. Nothing builds character in a worm like a good rototilling.

Some time ago a sporting-goods company sent me a package of freeze-dried worms. Honest. At first I thought it was some kind of veiled threat, but then I found a note saying that if I soaked the worms in water they would reconstitute into fishing bait. I stuck the package in my backpack with my other freeze-drieds and a couple of nights later at a mountain lake took it out and soaked the contents in some water. It turned out to be macaroni and cheese sauce. "That's funny," my friend Retch Sweeney said. "I thought we ate the macaroni and cheese sauce last night." The freeze-dried worms never did turn up.

The most troublesome of all live bait is the grasshopper. By the time you've caught enough of them you're usually too tired to go fishing. Furthermore, grasshoppers are not content simply to sit around in a bottle waiting to be fed to some fish. Once a worm is in the can, he pretty well knows his fate is sealed and will lie back and take it easy until his number comes up. Not so with grasshoppers. They are no sooner in the bottle than they're plotting their escape. Every time the lid is lifted to insert a new inmate, half a dozen of the others will try to make a break for it. While I was still a young boy, I learned that the only way to foil their escapes was to shake the bottle vigorously and then slip the new grasshopper in while the others were still dazed. What apparently happens is that the grasshoppers get high from the shaking and like it so much that after a while you can hardly chase them out of the bottle with a stick. They just lie on their backs, smiling. Of course this is confusing to the new grasshopper, who thinks he has been incarcerated with a bunch of degenerate insects who keep calling out, "C'mon, man, give us another shake!"

To my mind, the best live bait is the hellgrammite, an

insect that resides on streambeds and builds little cocoons for itself out of pebbles. Fish cannot resist them, in their shells or out. They are the salted peanuts of baits. Not long ago I was fishing a stream in Idaho and hadn't had a nibble all day. Then I discovered a nice patch of hellgrammites and within a half an hour had nearly filled my limit with plump cutthroat. There were a dozen or so other anglers on the stream, and they were so astonished at my success that they could not help expressing their awe by jovially threatening to slash my waders the next time I was in deep water. Finally, after I had creeled my final catch, a couple of them came over and demanded to know what I was using.

"These," I said.

"Jeez, those are ugly-looking things!" one of them said. "I almost hate to touch them."

"Trout love 'em," I said. "Here, take a couple of mine just to try them out." I thought it was the very least I could do.

As I was climbing into my car, I heard one of the other fishermen yell, "What was he using?"

"These nasty-looking things," the first fellow yelled back. "Big, red, white, and blue flies!"

I felt a little bad about the deception. On the other hand, you can never tell. There could be such a thing as patriotic fish.

The Green Box

☞ ☞ ☞ The other day I came home and found my wife cleaning out the garage. She was covered from one end to the other with dirt and cobwebs. Beads of sweat were dripping off the tip of her nose as she came staggering out of the garage carrying a huge green box in the general direction of the garbage cans.

"You shouldn't be doing that," I scolded.

"I shouldn't?" she said, putting the box down and massaging the small of her back with both hands.

"No, you shouldn't," I said. "I'm saving the stuff in that box. Now you carry it right back to where you found it."

I could tell I had hurt her feelings, partly because her eyes got all teary and her mouth formed into this cute little pout, but mostly because of the way she sprang forward and tried to crush my instep with her sneakers. After she had calmed down a bit, I explained to her that the box she was attempting to commit to oblivion was filled with priceless relics of my sporting youth.

"You must be thinking of some other box," she said. "I checked, and this one is just filled with a bunch of old junk."

"Ha!" I exclaimed, thrusting my hand into the box and withdrawing an artifact at random. "And just what do you call this?"

"Junk," she said.

"Well, it just so happens that this little metal band is a 1950 deer tag. This is the tag of my very first deer."

"You shot your first deer in 1950?"

"No, my very first deer got away that year, but this was its tag."

The deer tag tripped the hair trigger of my reminiscence mechanism, and suddenly the last hour of daylight was flitting away on the last day of deer season, 1950. I was crouched behind a log at the edge of an abandoned apple orchard on the side of a mountain. A quarter of a mile away, my very first deer and several others were meandering down a brushy slope in the general direction of the orchard. My hope was that they would step out into the orchard while there was still light enough to shoot. The only sounds were those of my own nervous breathing and Olga Bonemarrow's impatient popping of gum in my ear.

"Jeez, I'm freezing," Olga said in a nasty tone. "I don't know why I ever let you talk me into this."

"Shhhh!" I said. I slipped out of my mackinaw and told her to put it on over her own coat, which she did. I myself was wondering why I had talked Olga into coming along. As a matter of fact, I hadn't had to talk that much. Olga had stopped by my place just as I was getting ready to go hunting. All I had said to her was, "Hey, Olga, how'd you like to take a little ride up into the mountains with me?"

She had given me a long look. "What for?"

I smiled mischievously, an expression I had been attempting to perfect in front of my bedroom mirror for the past few days. "You'll find out," I said. "It's something you ain't never done before."

"I wouldn't bet on it," Olga said. "But okay."

It turned out that this was indeed Olga's first experience with hunting. She tried her best to conceal her surprise under a veneer of rage. Despite my best efforts to keep her quiet as we waited for my first deer to step into the orchard, she continued to growl and complain and whine, her hands thrust deep into the pockets of my mackinaw. In the thicket on the far side of the orchard, my straining eyes picked up a movement. Then a buck stepped halfway out of the brush and ran an inventory on the orchard. This was it. Tensely, I slipped the safety off my Marlin .32 Special.

"Hey," Olga said suddenly. "How do you unlock this dumb cheap bracelet?"

I looked at her in horror. Snapped shut around her wrist was my deer tag!

I stood up, slipped the rifle safety back on, and jacked out the shells. My first deer vanished in a single bound.

"How come your eyes are watering?" Olga said.

" 'Cause I'm cold," I said. "Give me back my mackinaw."

The sound of my wife's voice snapped me back to the present. "I don't know what's so great about an old deer tag," she said. "Look, it's even been snipped in two. Why would you lock it and then snip it in two if you never used it?"

There are certain things the female mind is incapable of fathoming, so I ignored the question. Rummaging around in the box, I found the first dry fly I ever tied and held it up for my wife to view. She screeched and jumped back.

"It's just a dry fly," I told her.

"Thank heavens!" she said. "I thought the cat had killed another bird."

"So, you're interested in birds, are you?" I said, pulling from the box one of my most prized treasures. "This is the first grouse I ever shot. I mounted it myself."

"Why, that's just some feathers glued on a board."

"Actually," I explained, "I was a little close to the grouse when I shot. That's all that was left. Anyway, I *think* that's all that was left."

It happened like this. I had pursued the grouse into a swamp near my home and had just stepped over a deep drainage ditch, my old double-barreled 12-gauge at the ready, when I spotted the grouse on a limb a scant twenty feet away. He spotted me too, revved his engine, and took off. I pointed the shotgun and fired, thereby learning once and for all the valuable lesson of having the butt of the stock pressed firmly against one's shoulder, not six inches away from it, at the moment one squeezes the trigger. Even so, I probably would have survived the impact a good deal better had not both barrels fired simultaneously. Upon regaining my senses, I immediately assumed I would spend the rest of my life with my right shoulder wrapped around my back in approximately the shape of a taco shell. What really scared me though was that I was cold all over, my vision was blurred, and I couldn't breathe. Then I realized that I was a five-foot-eight person standing in a six-foot-deep drainage ditch filled with green slime. I scrambled out of the drain ditch with the alacrity of a person who has a profound dread of green slime, and went in immediate pursuit of the grouse. A few feathers were still drifting in the air, but there was no other sign of the grouse. "I couldn't have missed at that range?" I mumbled, scarcely able to bring myself to accept the obvious. It was almost too sad even to think about. *I had vaporized my first grouse.* Glumly, I picked up as many feathers as I could find, took them home, and glued them on a board, printing neatly underneath them with lead pencil the words MY FIRST GROUSE, 1948.

"Maybe you just plain outright missed the grouse," my wife said. "Did you ever consider that possibility?"

"No, I would never consider that possibility," I informed her. "Anyhow, if I missed, it wouldn't have been my first grouse, would it? How do you explain that?"

While she was still struggling with this flawless bit of logic I extracted another relic from the green box. "Now this lovely piece of material is what remains of what once was one of my finest fishing hats. I called it my lucky hat."

"Looks like an old grease rag to me," my wife said.

"That's just because you don't have any true sense of aesthetics and . . . uh . . . say, this *is* a grease rag! How'd it get mixed in with these valuables? I bet I had you fooled when I let on like it was my lucky hat. Heh, heh."

"Heh, heh," she said without enthusiasm.

The next item extracted from the green box evoked a memory of high school. It was a moldy plug of tobacco, with one sizable chaw taken from a single corner.

In the days of my youth I spent a great deal of time in the company of an old woodsman by the name of Rancid Crabtree. He was my idol. More than anything I wanted to be like Rancid, a man who owned himself, who spent his life roaming the woods, hunting and fishing and trapping, almost always enjoying himself. I tried to emulate him in every way, and even went so far one time as to try a chaw of tobacco.

On that memorable occasion, some of the guys and I

were discussing deer-hunting tactics in the back of the
classroom while we waited for the teacher, Mrs. Axelrod,
to come in and start haranguing us about the French
Revolution, as if it had been our fault. I casually hauled
out my plug of tobacco, took a good healthy chaw, then
stuffed the plug back in my pocket. Not one of the guys
so much as blinked, but I could tell they were impressed.
At that moment Mrs. Axelrod sailed into the room and
ordered us to our seats. Since she didn't even allow gum
chewing in class, I decided I had better get rid of the
tobacco fast. So I swallowed it.

A few minutes later, it became apparent to me that
one does not actually get rid of a chaw of tobacco by
swallowing it. The chaw, in fact, was traveling up and
down my esophagus like a yo-yo on a short string, and
was giving every indication that it was about to reenter
society at any moment.

"Now, who can tell us the underlying causes of the
French Revolution?" Mrs. Axelrod asked. She looked at
me. "Pat."

I pointed a questioning finger to my chest, hoping to
delay answering until the chaw was on the downstroke.

"Yes, you, the green person with the bloated cheeks!"
Mrs. Axelrod snapped.

One second later I departed the room in a manner I
hoped was not totally without dignity but which was later
described to me by Peewee Thompson as a "sort of
greenish blur."

Peering into the green box, I could scarcely refrain from
emitting a shout of joy. There, nestled among such
collector's items as gopher traps, a single warped bear-
paw snowshoe, a rusty machete, a jungle hammock, a
collection of spent cartridges, a collection of dried toads,
a perforated canteen, a casting reel encased in a perma-

nent backlash, a dog harness made out of nylon stockings, and other rare and priceless mementos of my sporting youth, was without doubt what had to be the world's most powerful hand-held slingshot. I had thought the slingshot lost to posterity.

The slingshot had been designed and built by me at about age ten. I describe it as hand-held because later I also had built a more powerful slingshot, one that consisted of two live trees and a series of bicycle inner tubes. That slingshot almost earned the distinction of putting the first human into orbit, a kid by the name of Henry, who, when a gang of us stretched the inner tubes back to the limit of our combined strength, failed to hear the order "Fire!" Henry reported later that the lift-off actually had been a lot of fun, but he had run into difficulty at the termination of reentry.

The fork of the world's most powerful hand-held slingshot consisted of a Y-shaped section of trunk from a birch tree that I hacked down with my machete. The bands were made of strips cut from a tractor inner tube. These strips were then woven together in such a manner as to greatly increase their firing power. The pouch consisted of a tongue cut from a leather boot. Whomper, as I called the slingshot, was a magnificent and awesome instrument. Originally, my intention in building Whomper had been to hunt elk with it. I was disappointed to discover upon its completion, however, that, strain as I might, I could no more stretch the bands than if they had been made of cast iron. I considered this only a minor defect, however, and took to carrying Whomper about with me in a special holster attached to the back of my belt. I also carried a regular slingshot for utilitarian and sporting purposes. It was this combination of elastic armaments that resulted in one of my more satisfying experiences as a youngster.

My old woodsman friend Rancid Crabtree had taken
me to the Loggers Picnic, an annual event in which the
loggers competed in eating, drinking, and feats of
strength. Rancid said he figured he could hold his own in
two of the categories but that he was too old and feeble
for feats of strength.

"Ah'll leave the feats of strangth to you," Rancid told
me.

Actually, I figured I might do quite well in some of
the events, but I was immediately sent to humiliating
defeat in arm wrestling by the strapping offspring of a
logger.

Rancid tried to console me. "Don't fret about it," he
said. "Some of them girls is a lot stronger than they look.
You'd a probly won iffin she'd been a boy."

No doubt my defeat by Mary Jane Railbender would
have gone unnoticed by most of the picnickers had it not
been for the presence of a large, loud, loathsome fellow
by the name of Whitey. Whitey, though ten years older
than myself, was one of my most despised enemies and
passed up no opportunity to torment me.

"Har, har, har!" he roared. "Got beat by a little snip
of a girl, did you? Har, har, har!" He then rushed to
spread the news among the loggers and their kin, who,
while they didn't exactly find the news of my downfall
sidesplitting, seemed at least mildly amused. To me, that
constituted excessive mirth at my expense, and I stalked
off beyond the reach of their har, har's.

While I was drowning my sorrow in a bottle of
orange crush, I happened to notice a flock of crows flying
over. As was my practice in those days, I sprang to my
feet, drew my regular slingshot to its full capacity, and let
fly at them with a rock. I missed the crows by a quarter of
a mile, but suddenly somebody yelled out, "Holy cow!
Who threw that rock? That's one heck of a throw!"

"That was just Pat," somebody else said. "But he done it with a slingshot."

"A slingshot!" shouted out Whitey. "Pat's got a slingshot? Must be made out of wishbone and a rubberband if he can shoot it, anybody who lets himself get beat by a little girl in arm wrastlin'." Whitey took the little sounds of amusement from the other picnickers for encouragement. "Here, Shrimpy, toss me yore peashooter. I'll show you how a man does with a slingshot."

From deep inside me I could feel this great, evil, hysterical laugh welling up, but I fought it back down. Calmly, with just the right touch of nonchalance, I reached behind me and drew Whomper from its holster. The big slingshot landed with a solid *chunk* at Whitey's feet. He stared down at it: the massive fork, the woven rubber bands thick as a man's wrist, the boot-tongue pouch, all of it bound together with wrappings of baling wire. Even from where I stood I could tell he was impressed.

"C'mon, Whitey," shouted Rancid from the crowd of spectators. "Show us how a man does with a slangshot!"

"All right, I will," said Whitey, and he scooped up the slingshot, fitted a stone the size of a walnut in the pouch, and hauled back. Well, it was a terrible spectacle to have to witness, and I've always felt a little remorseful that I enjoyed it so much. Up to the part where the buttons started popping off the front of Whitey's shirt and flying about like shrapnel, I thought Whitey might actually stretch the sling an inch or two. But by the time the women and little children were sent away because of the horrible sounds he was making, I knew there wasn't a chance.

At last, quivering with rage and exhaustion, Whitey threw the slingshot to the ground. "Ain't nobody can pull that thing," he gasped. For a second, I thought I detected a wave of sympathy, even admiration, flowing from the spectators toward Whitey.

Then Rancid stepped forward. "Shucks," he said. "Let a feeble old man give thet thang a try." He grabbed up Whomper, hauled back until the woven tractor-tube bands hummed like guitar strings. He then shot the rock out of sight. His face split in a big grin, Rancid handed Whomper back to me. The loggers laughed and applauded and slapped both me and Rancid on the back. I never again had any trouble from Whitey.

When we were driving home, Rancid still had the big grin on his face.

"What's so funny?" I asked him.

"Ain't nuthin' funny," he said through his teeth.

"How come you're grinning like that then?"

"Ah ain't grinnin'," he said. "Ah thank Ah ruptured maw face pullin' thet dang slangshot!"

My wife kicked the green box with one of her sneakers. "All right, all right, I won't throw this junk out if it means so much to you that you have to reminisce for twenty minutes over every piece of it."

"What?" I said. "No, of course you're not going to throw it out. I won't let you. Say, look at this! Look at the stuff in this jar. It's some of my old bear grease!"

"Oh, good heavens," she said. "Now I suppose you're going to tell me how you used to grease bears."

That really burned me up. Who would have thought she would guess the punch line of one of my best stories?

Skunk Dog

☞ ☞ ☞**W**hen I was a kid, I used to beg my mother to get me a dog.

"You've got a dog," she would say.

"No, I mean a real dog," I'd reply.

"Why, you've got Strange, and he's a real dog, more or less."

Strange was mostly less. He had stopped by to cadge a free meal off of us one day and found the pickings so easy he decided to stay on. He lived with us for ten years, although, as my grandmother used to say, it seemed like centuries. In all those years, he displayed not a single socially redeeming quality. If dogs were films, he'd have been X-rated.

I recall one Sunday when my mother had invited the new parish priest to dinner. Our dining room table was situated in front of a large window overlooking the front yard. During the first course, Strange passed by the window not once but twice, walking on his front legs but dragging his rear over the grass. His mouth was split in an ear-to-ear grin of sublime relief, and possibly of pride, in his discovery of a new treatment for embarrassing itch.

"Well, Father," Mom said in a hasty effort at distraction, "and how do you like our little town by now?"

"Hunh?" the pastor said, a fork full of salad frozen in mid-stroke as he gaped out the window at the disgusting spectacle. "Pardon me, what were you saying?"

During the next course, Strange appeared outside the window with the remains of some creature that had met its end sometime prior to the previous winter, no doubt something he had saved for just such a formal occasion. As he licked his chops in pretense of preparing to consume the loathsome object, Mom shot me a look that said, "*Kill that dog!*" I stepped to the door fully intending to carry out the order, but Strange ran off, snickering under his breath.

"More chicken, Father?" Mom asked.

"Thank you, I think not," the priest said, running a finger around the inside of his Roman collar, as if experiencing some welling of the throat.

Fortunately, the dinner was only four courses in length, ending before Strange could stage his grand finale. A female collie, three dead rats, and the entrails of a sheep were left waiting in the wings.

Mom said later she didn't know whether Strange was just being more disgusting than usual that day or had something against organized religion. In any case, it was a long while before the priest came to dinner again, our invitations invariably conflicting with funerals, baptisms, or his self-imposed days of fasting.

Strange was the only dog I've ever known who could belch at will. It was his idea of high comedy. If my mother had some of her friends over for a game of pinochle, Strange would slip into the house and slouch over to the ladies. Then he would emit a loud belch. Apparently, he mistook shudders of revulsion for a form of applause, because he would sit there on his haunches, grinning modestly up at the group and preparing an encore. "Stop, stop!" he would snarl, as I dragged him back outdoors. "They love me! They'll die laughing at my other routine! It'll have them on the floor!" I will not speak here of his other routine.

In general appearance, Strange could easily have been mistaken for your average brown-and-white mongrel with floppy ears and a shaggy tail, except that depravity was written all over him. He looked as if he sold dirty postcards to support an opium habit. His eyes spoke of having known the depths of degeneracy, and approving of them.

Tramps were his favorite people. If a tramp stopped by for a free meal at our picnic table and to case the place, Strange would greet him warmly, exchange bits of news about underworld connections, and leak inside information about the household: "They ain't got any decent jewelry, but the silver's not bad and there's a good radio in the living room." The tramp would reach down and scratch the dog behind the ears as a gesture of appreciation, and Strange would belch for him. Face wrinkled in disgust, the tramp would then hoist his bedroll and depart the premises, no doubt concerned about the reliability of food given him by a family that kept such a dog.

My friends at school often debated the attributes of various breeds of dogs. "I tend to favor black labs," I'd say, going on to recite the various characteristics I had recently excerpted from a *Field & Stream* dog column. Somehow my classmates got the impression that I actually owned a black lab and had personally observed these characteristics. While I was aware of the mistaken impression, I didn't feel it was my business to go around refuting all the rumors that happened to get started.

Sooner or later, however, one of these friends would visit me at home. Strange would come out of his house and satisfy himself that the visitor wasn't a tramp in need of his counsel. That done, he would yawn, belch, gag, and return to his den of iniquity.

"That your uh dog?" the kid would ask.

"I guess so," I'd reply, embarrassed.

"Too bad," the kid would say. "I always thought you had a black lab."

"Naw, just him. But I'm planning on buying me a black lab pup first chance I get."

"I sure would," the kid would say, shaking his head.

As a hunting dog, Strange was a good deal worse than no dog. Nevertheless, he clearly thought of himself as a great hunting guide. "Fresh spoor," he would say, indicating a pine cone. "We can't be far behind him. And for gosh sakes shoot straight, because I judge from the sign he'll be in a bad mood!"

Chances of shooting any game at all with Strange along were nil. He had no concept of stealth. His standard hunting practice was to go through the woods shouting directions and advice to me and speculating loudly about the absence of game. I would have had more luck hunting with a rock band.

Strange did not believe in violence, except possibly in regard to chickens. He couldn't stand chickens. If a chicken walked by his house, Strange would rush out in a rage and tell the bird off and maybe even cuff it around a bit in the manner of early Bogart or Cagney. "You stupid chicken, don't ever let me catch you in dis neighborhood again, you hear?"

Some of our neighbors kept half-starved timber wolves for watchdogs. Occasionally one of these beasts would come loping warily through our yard and encounter Strange. Since Strange considered the whole world as his territory, he felt no particular obligation to defend this small portion of it. He would sit there, figuratively picking his teeth with a match, and stare insolently at the wolf, who was four times his size, its lip curled over glistening fangs, hackles raised, growls rumbling up from its belly. After a bit, the wolf would circle Strange, back away, and then lope on, occasionally casting a nervous glance back over its shoulder. "Punk!" Strange would mutter. Probably the reason none of these wolves ever attacked Strange was that they figured he was carrying a switchblade and maybe a blackjack.

Despite the peculiar passive side to his character, Strange did commit a single act of violence that was so terrible my mother actually considered selling the farm and moving us all to town. At the very least, she said, she was getting rid of Strange.

The episode began one warm spring evening when my grandmother sighted a skunk scurrying under our woodshed.

"He's probably the one that's been killing our chickens," Gram said. "I wouldn't be surprised but that he has his missus under there and they're planning a family. We'll be overrun with skunks!"

"Well, we'll just have to get him out from under the woodshed," Mom said. "Land sakes, a person can scarcely get a breath of fresh air in the backyard without smelling skunk. Maybe we should get Rancid Crabtree to come over and see what he can do about it."

"He'd certainly overpower the skunk smell," Gram said, "but I don't see that's any gain."

"What I mean is," Mom said, "maybe Rancid could trap the skunk or at least get it to leave. It's worth a try."

"I don't know," Gram said. "It just doesn't seem like a fair contest to me."

"Because Rancid uses guns and traps?" I asked.

"No, because the skunk has a brain!"

Gram and Rancid were not fond of each other.

The next day I was sent to tell Rancid we needed his expertise in extracting a skunk from under our wood-shed. His face brightened at this news.

"Ha!" he said. "Thet ol' woman couldn't figure out how to git a skonk out from under yore shed, so fust thang she does is start yelling fer ol' Crabtree! If thet don't beat all!"

"Actually, it was Mom who told me to come get you," I said.

"Oh. Wall, in thet case, Ah'll come. Jist keep the ol' woman outta ma ha'r."

When we arrived, Gram was standing out by the woodshed banging on a pot with a steel spoon and whooping and hollering. The old woodsman nudged me in the ribs and winked. I could tell he was going to get off one of his "good ones."

"Would you mind practicin' your drummin' and singin' somewhar else?" Rancid said to her. "Me and the boy got to git a skonk out from under thet shed."

If Gram could have given the skunk the same look she fired at Rancid, the creature would have been stunned if not killed outright. The glare had no effect on Rancid, however, since he was bent over laughing and slapping his knee in appreciation of his good one. It was, in fact, one of the best good ones I'd ever heard him get off, but I didn't dare laugh.

"All right, Bob Hope," Gram snapped. "Let's see how you get the skunk out from under there. Maybe if you stood upwind of it, that would do the trick!"

"Don't rile me, ol' woman, don't rile me," Rancid said. "Now, boy, go fetch me some newspapers. Ah'm gonna smoke thet critter outta thar."

"And burn down the shed most likely," Gram said.

"Ha!" Rancid said. "You thank Ah don't know how to smoke a skonk out from under a shed?"

Fortunately, the well and a bucket were close at hand and we were able to douse the fire before it did any more damage than blackening one corner of the building.

During these proceedings, Strange had emerged from his house and sat looking on with an air of bemusement. There was nothing he loved better than a ruckus.

"Maybe we should just let the skunk be," Mom said.

"Land sakes, yes!" Gram shouted at Rancid. "Before you destroy the whole dang farm!"

Rancid snorted. "No skonk's ever bested me yet, and this ain't gonna be the fust!"

After each failed attempt to drive out the skunk, Rancid seemed to become angrier and more frenzied. Furiously, he dug a hole on one side of the shed. Then he jammed a long pole in through the hole and flailed wildly about with it. No luck. He went inside the shed and jumped up and down on the floor with his heavy boots. Still no skunk emerged. At one point, he tried to crawl under the shed, apparently with the idea of entering into hand-to-gland combat with the skunk, but the shed floor was too low to the ground. Then he grabbed up the pole and flailed it wildly under the floor again. Next he dropped the pole and yelled at me, "Go git another batch of newspapers!"

"No, no, no!" screamed Mom.

"Leave the poor skunk alone," Gram yelled. "I'm startin' to become fond of the little critter!"

Rancid stood there panting and mopping sweat from his forehead with his arm. "Ah know what Ah'll do, Ah'll set a trap fer him! Should of did thet in the fust place. No skonk is gonna . . ."

At that moment, the skunk, no doubt taking advantage of the calm, or perhaps frightened by it, ran out from under the shed and made for the nearby brush.

"Ah figured thet little trick would work," Rancid said, although no one else was quite sure which trick he was speaking of. "And this way, there ain't no big stank, which is how Ah planned it."

Then Strange tore into the skunk.

The battle was short but fierce, with the skunk expending its whole arsenal as Strange dragged it about the yard, up the porch and down, into the woodshed and out, and through the group of frantically dispersing spectators. At last, coming to his senses, the dog dropped the skunk and allowed it to stagger off into the bushes.

Strange seemed embarrassed by his first and only display of heroism. "I don't know what came over me," he said, shaking. "I've got nothing against skunks!" Still, I couldn't help but be proud of him.

The skunk was gone, but its essence lingered on. The air was stiff with the smell of skunk for weeks afterwards.

"That dog has got to go," Mom said. But, of course, Strange refused to go, and that was that.

It was years before Strange was entirely free of the skunk odor. Every time he got wet, the smell came back in potent force.

"Phew!" a new friend of mine would say. "That your dog?"

"Yeah," I'd say, proudly, "he's a skunk dog."

Cold Fish

☞ ☞ ☞ **S**how me a man who fishes in winter, and I'll show you a fanatic. Actually, I'll get the better of the deal, because for sheer spectacle a fanatic doesn't hold a candle to a man who fishes in winter.

I have often thought that if you could capture a half-dozen winter fishermen and put them in a circus sideshow you could make a fortune on them: "Step right this way ladies and gentlemen—no children please, we don't want to warp any young minds—and see the men who actually fish during the winter! They are amazing, they are absolutely astounding! Their skin is blue, their hair is blue, ladies and gentlemen, even their *language* is blue!"

Much as it pains me, I must confess that I too am a winter fisherman. It has been said that the first step toward recovering from this affliction is to admit that you are one, but I have been admitting it for years without noticeable effect. Actually, I take a certain pride in being a member of this select but compulsive group of hearty anglers. We even have a number of sayings: "No man is an icicle unto himself, but each a piece of the whole cube." And: "If one ice fisherman is defrosted, another will freeze to take his place." This goes to show that you can't expect memorable sayings from a bunch of demented fishermen.

Frequently I am asked why a man of my age and character persists in fishing right on through the most bitter months of winter. If I recall correctly, the exact wording of the question is: "Why does an old fool like you persist in going fishing in sub-zero weather?"

My answer is succinct and to the point. "Shut up and help me off with these *bleeping* boots. And be careful with my socks! I don't want my toes falling out and rolling under the chesterfield!"

There is a thin streak of sadism that runs through the directors of state fish and game departments. I have long suspected the requirements for fish and game directors include the following: "Must be outstanding citizens of their communities; must have demonstrated deep interest in outdoor sports and recreation; must have not less than three years experience as fiends."

How else explain their declaring certain waters open during the winter months? Indeed, I have no difficulty imagining the directors roaring with maniacal laughter as they debate the subject of which waters to open for winter fishing.

"Hey, fellows," says Milt Thumbscrew, "how about opening Lake Chill Factor during February?" He giggles wildly.

The other directors stomp their feet and pound on the table as they try to withdraw from fits of hysterical laughter.

"Oh dear, that's absolutely great!" says Adolf Wrinklebunn. "Can't you just see those poor devils up to their armpits in snow and ice, fighting their way to the lake!" He slides from his chair, shrieking.

"And they aren't even out of their cars yet!" screams the chairman. "Oh, stop, stop, you're killing me! Quick, somebody call for the vote!"

Now, even though I know that is basically how and why certain water is open for winter fishing, I find the enticement almost impossible to resist. Consider, if you will, a telephone conversation I had with my friend Retch Sweeney a while back.

"Speak up," I said. "The wind is howling so bad outside I can't hear you."

"I said," Retch shouted, "I tried to get through to you earlier, but the lines were down. I guess the ice got so heavy on them they broke. Anyway, I got this terrible urge to go fishing."

"Well, that's easily cured," I said. "Just go out in your backyard and stand in a bucket of ice water while your wife shovels snow down the back of your neck."

"I already tried that, but I still got the urge," Retch said.

"Have you talked to a psychiatrist?"

"As a matter of fact I did. I ran into Doc Portnoy over at the hospital. He was the one who told me about catching a five-pound rainbow up on the Frigid River. It's open in February, ya know."

"A five-pounder! Did he say what he caught it on?"

"Salmon eggs. That was all I could get out of him before the nurses rushed him into the furnace room in a last-ditch effort to thaw him out."

"I'll get my gear together and pick you up in half an hour," I said. Actually, it took me a bit longer than I had anticipated. I hadn't figured in the time it would take to stand in a bucket of ice water in the backyard while my wife shoveled snow down the back of my neck.

When I was a kid still in my single-digit years, I got my start in winter fishing under the tutelage of old Rancid Crabtree. Rancid was a man who believed in teaching a kid the basics.

"You know how to check fer thin ice, boy?" he would ask me. "Wall, what you do is stick one foot way out ahead of you and stomp the ice real hard and listen fer it to make a crackin' sound. Thar now, did you hear how the ice cracked whan Ah stomped it? Thet means it's too thin to hold a man's weight. Now pull me up out of hyar and we'll run back to shore and see if we kin built a fahr b'fore Ah freezes to death!"

Our usual practice was simply to hike out on the frozen surface of the lake or river, chop a hole in the ice, and try to catch some fish before either the hole or we froze over. One year, however, we built ourselves a luxurious fishing shack. It was made of scrap lumber, rusty tin, tarpaper, and other equally attractive materials. We put a tiny airtight heater inside with the stovepipe running out through the roof at a rakish angle. I always expected the stovepipe to set fire to the roof and was not often disappointed. Having the roof catch fire became so much a part of our fishing routine that Rancid would say to me, "Go put the fahr on the roof out, will ya? Ah thank Ah jist had a bite."

The truth is I was always glad for an excuse to step outside of the shack for a breath of fresh air. Rancid was a man who bathed only on leap years, and the previous leap year had escaped his notice. He smelled bad enough dry; wet, he could drive a lame badger out of its hole at forty yards. Sometimes in the warmth of the tiny shack he would actually begin to steam, and that was the worst. I'd sit there hoping the roof would catch fire so I'd have an excuse to step outside.

Sometimes when I knew I'd be cooped up in the

fishing shack with Rancid for several hours on the
following day, I'd try to induce in him the desire to take a
bath.

"You know what I like to do after a nasty chore like
this," I'd tell him as we worked together at his place. "I
like to climb into a nice hot tub of soapy water and soak
and scrub and soak and scrub and soak and scrub.
Doesn't that sound good?"

"Nope, it don't. Now watch what yore doin' thar!
How many times I got to show you how to skin a skonk?"

Despite Rancid's aversion to bathing, the days we
spent fishing together in the fish shack were among the
best I've ever known. From the darkness of the shack you
could peer through the hole in the ice clear down to the
bottom of the lake and watch the fish move in to take the
bait. And Rancid would tell me all the old stories over
again, changing them just enough each time so that they
always seemed fresh and new. He gave me little fishing
tips, too. He said one good way to warm up bait maggots
was to stick a pinch of them under your lower lip. I said
I'd have to try that sometime when the need arose. After
thirty years and more, the need has not yet arisen, but it's
a good thing to know anyhow.

Another interesting thing he told me was about the
time he went fishing in winter and it was so cold his line
froze right in the middle of a cast. He said it was
downright comical the way his line just stuck out in the air
stiff as a wire from the end of his pole. He had to stand
his line up against a tall snag and build a little fire near it.
As the end close to the fire thawed out, the line just slid
down the snag and formed itself into a nice little coil.
Rancid knew all kinds of neat fishing lore like that.

The one problem with the fishing shack was that
dragging it about the lake from one fishing site to
another bore a striking resemblance to hard work.

Rancid said that he didn't have anything against hard work in principle and that if other folks wanted to indulge themselves in it that was all right with him and he certainly wouldn't hold it against them. He said that some folks were born with that flaw in their character and just couldn't help themselves. All a decent man could do, he said, was pretend that such folks were just as normal as anybody else and that they should never be looked down upon or ridiculed or in any way be made to feel inferior.

Rancid told me that what a normal man did when confronted with a task that bore a striking resemblance to hard work was to sit down and try to come up with an idea for avoiding it. That is exactly what Rancid did in regard to the fishing shack.

"Ah got a great idea," he said. "What we is gonna do is rig up a sail fer the fish shack! We'll let the wind blow the fish shack along the ice and we'll jist foller along behind and steer it whar ever we wants it to go."

In practically no time at all, Rancid had a tall, slender cedar pole bolted to the front end of the fish shack for a mast. A massive canvas tarp was converted swiftly into a sail. A confusion of booms, lines, and pulleys allowed the sail to be hauled up the mast, in which position its general appearance was not unlike some of the sails on the boats pictured in my geography book.

"Say, it looks just like a Chinese junk," I told Rancid, realizing at once that I had hurt his feelings.

"Ah don't care iffin it looks like a whole gol-durn Chinese dump," he snapped, "jist so it works."

Looking back through the corrective lens of time, I now realize that Rancid was one of those men who just can't let a good idea be but have to keep improving on it right up to the point where it turns into a catastrophe. I didn't know that back then, of course, and just assumed that what happened was one of those unavoidable mishaps that occurred with surprising regularity while I was in the company of Rancid.

Much to my surprise, the sail worked like a charm. The gentle breeze on the lake filled the billowing tarp and moved the little fish shack steadily if somewhat jerkily across the wind-burnished surface of the ice. We walked behind or alongside the shack, guiding the little vessel this way and that by pulling on various lines, much as one guides horses with a set of reins. Then Rancid came up with his improvement on the basic idea.

"Say," he said, "Ah got me a good notion to get inside the shack and jist ride along. Ah bet Ah kin steer it jist by pushing a stick along the ice through the hole in the floor. Iffin the critter gits to movin' too fast, Ah'll jist drag maw feet to slow it down."

The breeze had fallen off for the moment, so we made fast all the lines and Rancid climbed into the shack and made himself comfortable. Later Rancid was to accuse me of having dropped the spike through the latch on the outside of the door, thereby locking him inside; but if that was the case, the action was merely an absentminded reflex on my part and bore not the slightest hint of mischief. Besides, how was I to know that anytime he wanted out I wouldn't be there to pull the spike out of the latch?

I stood around outside the shack stomping my feet and rubbing my hands together, waiting for a breeze to come up and get us under way again. Every so often, Rancid would shout at me from inside the shack. "Any sign of wind out thar yet?"

"Nope," I'd reply. "It's pretty quiet." If I'd been more attuned to the weather, I would have known that the particular quiet we were experiencing was the kind known as "ominous."

I heard a distant rustling behind me. Turning, I observed a rather startling phenomenon. Clouds of snow were billowing up off the far side of the lake and moving in our direction.

"HOLY COW, RANCID, THE WIND . . . !"

"The wind's comin' up is she? Hot dang! Now yore gonna see . . ."

He never finished his sentence.

As soon as I got to my feet after being knocked down by the first blast of wind, I tried to track the fish shack as best I could. I felt I owed it to Rancid, since by then I had remembered dropping the spike through the latch. Rancid wasn't a person you wanted to have mad at you.

For a long ways, I could see the skid marks Rancid had made with his boots on the ice. After that I saw some scratches that looked like they had been made by two sets of fingernails. Then there were only the ski marks made by the sled and an occasional board or piece of tin from the fish shack. Over several long stretches, where the shack had become airborne, there were no signs at all.

After a while I came across two ice fishermen fighting against the wind on their way home. I asked them if they had seen Rancid go by in the fish shack. They said they had.

"I don't know what that durn fool will think of next," one of the men said, "but he was reachin' out a little winder with a hatchet, and it looked like he was tryin' to chop down the pole holdin' up that hay tarp. He went by so fast we couldn't rightly see what he was up to."

"Did you hear him say anything?" I asked.

"Nothin' I'd repeat to a boy your age," the man said.

A half-mile farther on, I ran into another fisherman. Before I could ask him anything, he said, "Land sakes, boy, you shouldn't be out alone in a blizzard like this! Why, I just saw some farmer's hay tarp fly by here.

Somehow it got hooked onto his outhouse and was draggin' it along too. Just tearin' that privy all to pieces. Strangest dang thing I ever seen! Anyway, come along with me and I'll give you a ride home."

I was about to refuse, when I glanced off across the lake and saw the figure of a tall, lean man striding purposefully in our direction through the clouds of driven snow. Even though he was downwind from me, I could tell it was Rancid. I could also tell he was carrying what looked like a piece of broken ski in one hand.

"I'll ride home with you on one condition," I told the fisherman. "And that is that you leave right now."

The Rifle

☞ ☞ ☞At least once a week from the fifth grade on, I made it a practice to stop by Clyde Fitch's Sport Shop after school. Clyde was always glad to see me, and we would josh each other.

"Hi, Clyde," I'd say as I came through the door.

"Don't handle the guns," Clyde would say.

"Yeah, there is a chill in the air," I'd respond. "Folks say it's gonna be an early winter."

"You got peanut butter on one of the twelve-gauges last time," he would retort. "I wish you'd find someplace else to eat your after-school snack."

I would nod appreciatively at Clyde's sharp wit and mark up a score for him in the air. Then, as he turned to wait on a customer, I would hear a soft sweet song beckoning me to the gun racks. It would be the rifles and shotguns singing to me:

"You drive me to distraction

When you work my lever action," sang a .30-30.

"When you give my stock a nuzzle,

You send chills down to my muzzle," trilled a .270.

"I lie awake nights
After you peer down my sights," moaned a .30-06.

I'll admit they weren't great lyricists, but they had nice voices and the melody was pleasant. Before I knew what was happening, a .30-06 would have leaped into my hands and I would be checking its action.

"DON'T TOUCH THE GUNS!" Clyde Fitch would yell, doing a fair impression of an enraged businessman.

"Good, Clyde, good," I would say as I set the rifle back in the rack and peered down at a sleek, inviting .300. Apparently displeased by my lack of enthusiasm for his performance, Clyde would rush over, grab me by the back of my coat collar and belt, and rush me out the door of his establishment. We kidded around with each other like that for about four years, occasionally working in new bits of dialogue but with Clyde always opening with his favorite line, "Don't touch the guns!" I suppose the reason he liked it so much was that it always got a laugh.

Just a few days short of eternity, my fourteenth birthday finally arrived. I had expected it to come bearing as a gift one .30-30 rifle, about which I had dropped approximately 30,000 hints to my family. No rifle! I could tell from the shapes of the packages. They were all shaped like school clothes. "Something seems to be missing here," I said, nervously ripping open a package of Jockey shorts. "You sure you didn't forget and leave one of my presents in the closet?"

"No," my mother said. "That's the whole kit and kaboodle of them right there."

"I was, uh, sort of expecting a, uh, thirty-thirty rifle."

"Oh," Mom said. "Well, if you want a rifle, you'll just have to get yourself a job and earn enough money to buy one."

It was not unusual in those days for parents to say brutal things like that to their children. There were no laws back then to prevent parents from saying no and, worse yet, meaning no. Life was hard for a kid. Still, I couldn't believe that my mother was actually suggesting that her only son go out and find a job.

"Surely you are jesting," I said to her.

"No," she replied.

Naturally, I had heard about work. My family was always talking about it within range of my hearing, and, as far as I could tell, seemed generally to be in favor of it. I didn't know why. Nothing I ever heard about work made it seem very appealing. My old friend Rancid Crabtree had told me that he had tried work once as a young man. He said that he was supposed to cut down trees for the man who had hired him, but when he picked up the ax and started to chop, his whole life passed before him. He gave up work then and there. He said that he knew some folks loved to work, and that was fine, but that he himself couldn't stand even to be near it. Of the two opinions about work, I favored Rancid's.

Still, if I wanted to hunt deer that coming fall, I would need a rifle. On the other hand, if I got a job, that would ruin my summer and leave me only mornings and evenings and weekends to fish. At best, I might be able to get in some more fishing on days I was too sick to work. I weighed my need for the rifle against a ruined summer and, after much long and painful thought, arrived at a distasteful decision: I would have to borrow a rifle.

Then, as now, people did not stand in line to loan out their rifles to beginning hunters, or to anyone else for that matter. Rancid Crabtree seemed to me to be the best prospect for the loan of a rifle.

"By the way, Rancid," I said to him casually one day, "how about loaning me your thirty-thirty for deer season this year."

Rancid's face erupted into that beautiful snaggletoothed grin of his. "Thet's a good-un," he said. "Make it up yersef or somebody tell it to you?"

"It's no joke," I said. "I need a deer rifle, and I don't see why you can't loan me your thirty-thirty."

"Wall, Ah would loan it to you except fer one thang," Rancid said. "An' thet is, Ah don't want to."

Rancid had only two defects to his character: He had never learned the art of mincing words, and you could never talk him into doing something he didn't want to do.

I shook my head in despair. "You're the only person I can think of, Rancid, who might loan me a rifle. I guess the only thing left for me to do is to get a job and earn some money."

"Now don't go talkin' like thet," Rancid said, as soon as he had recovered from the shock. "A young fella like you, got everthang to live fer, talkin' about gettin' a j-j-jo—throwin' away his life. No sar, Ah won't stand fer it! Now, hyar's what you do. You go ask the Inyun if you kin borry one of his rifles."

"Pinto Jack?"

"Why shore, ol' Pinto'd give you the hide offen his scrawny carcass iffin it had a zipper on it."

I found Pinto Jack puffing a pipe on the front porch of his cabin, and put my request straight to him.

Pinto Jack smiled only on rare occasions, and this was not one of them. "You want to borrow my rifle?" he said, studying me thoughtfully through a cloud of pipe smoke. "If I loaned you my rifle, what would I use when I raided the ranchers and burned their buildings and drove off their livestock, and like that?"

"Couldn't you use a bow and arrow for a few raids?" I said.

"You tell me, how am I going to drive my old truck and shoot a bow and arrow at the same time? No, I got to have my rifle for raiding the ranchers."

I looked crestfallen, having many years before learned that this was one of the best looks to use on Pinto Jack.

"Tell you what," he said after a moment. "I could maybe let you use the old rifle my father brought back from the Great War."

"First World?"

"Little Big Horn. It's a single-shot and kicks a bit, but you're welcome to it."

I rushed home lugging the monstrous firearm, pinned a target to a fence post backed by a sandbank, paced off a hundred yards, drew a bead on the target, and gently squeezed the trigger. Later I heard that all the livestock within a mile radius sprang two feet into the air and went darting about in all directions at that altitude. Apples rained down out of the trees in the orchards. Three lumberjacks swore off drink, and two atheists were converted to religion. My own interpretation of the event was that I had just been struck by lightning, a meteorite, or a bomb. When my vision cleared, I knew I was in trouble. Not only would my folks be upset about my shooting one of their fence posts in half, but the neighbors would be mad at me for destroying their sandbank. Nevertheless, I decided to try one more shot, this one left-handed. The second shot went off a little better, since by now I knew what to expect. It was easier for me to keep my nose out of the way, too, because the first shot had moved it up into the vacant area above my right eyebrow where it would be safe. By the time I had finished sighting in the rifle, I figured I'd be the only kid in the school talent show who could applaud behind his back with his shoulder blades.

My first deer managed to elude me that year. Even though I had opportunities for several good shots, by the time I had grimaced enough to pull the trigger, the deer was always gone. At the end of the season, I returned the rifle to Pinto Jack.

"Any luck?" he asked.

"Nope."

"Well, don't feel so bad about it," he said. "Come on in and have yourself an orange pop, and I'll show you how I can applaud with my shoulder blades. Bet you don't know anybody who can do that."

By the time the next summer rolled around, it had become apparent to me that the only way I was ever going to get a deer rifle was to earn the money for it. There was a dairy farmer by the name of Brown who lived nearby and whose reputation in the community was that of a kindly, if somewhat frugal, gentleman. Out of desperation for a deer rifle, I broke down and indentured myself to him at the rate of fifty cents an hour manufacturing postholes. Mr. Brown gave me the job after asking if I thought I could do a man's work. My ingenious reply was: "It depends on the man." The farmer said later that he supposed the particular man I had been referring to was an Egyptian mummy. For all his other drawbacks, Mr. Brown did not lack a sense of humor.

About his other drawbacks. It was only after going to work for him that I discovered that he wasn't a kindly gentleman at all but the former commandant of a slave-labor camp. Our mutual misfortune was that he had somehow missed the last boat to Brazil and had been forced to escape to Idaho, where he took up dairy farming as a cover.

"Vork, vork!" he would scream at me, slapping the leg of his bib overalls with a swagger stick. "Make die postholes, make die postholes, fahster, fahster!"

And I would streak about the landscape, trailing fresh-dug postholes. Sometimes, after glancing nervously around, I would step behind a tree to catch my breath. The farmer would drop out of the branches and screech at me: "Vot you do-ink? I not pay-ink you fifty zents an hour to breathe! Vork! Vork!"

At day's end, my mother would drive over to the farm to give me a ride home. She and the farmer would chat about my capacity for hard labor.

"I'm surprised you can get any work out of him at all," Mom would say.

The old farmer would laugh in his kindly way. "Actually, I have found him to be a bit slow, but he is doing better. Just today, while he was digging a posthole, I thought I detected some motion in one of his arms." Then he would give me a pat on my sagging, quivering back. "Off you go now, lad. See you bright and early in the morning!"

Odd, I thought. He seems to have lost his accent.

Bright and early the next morning the farmer would tell me: "Vork, vork, lazy Dummkopf! Make die postholes, fahster, fahster!"

At the end of the very hour in which I earned the last fifty cents I needed to buy the rifle, I resigned my position. When I told the farmer I was quitting, he tried to conceal his disappointment by leaping in the air and clicking his heels. There are few things, by the way, more disgusting than a dairy farmer clicking his heels in the air.

"I'll say this for you," he told me. "You have dug what I regard to be the most expensive postholes in the whole history of agriculture. If it was possible, I would gather them all up and put them in a bank vault rather than leave them scattered randomly about my property. Nevertheless, lad, should you ever find yourself in need of a job to buy yourself, say, a shotgun, why you just come to me. I'll be happy to recommend you as a worker to my neighbor, Fergussen, who, though I may say a harsh word about him now and again, is not a bad sort at all, particularly for a man who is stupid and greedy and probably a thief."

Naturally, I was flattered by this little farewell speech. I even changed my mind about his being a former commandant of a slave-labor camp. "Thanks," I told him, "but now that I've tried work and found it to be about what I expected, I think I'll avoid it in the future."

Mr. Brown said he thought that would be a good idea and that, as far as he had observed, I had considerable talent for that line of endeavor and was practically assured of success.

The very next day, with the money for the rifle wadded up in a pocket of my jeans, I sauntered into Clyde Fitch's Sport Shop.

"Hi, Clyde," I said.

"Don't touch the guns!" Clyde shouted.

I took out my wad of money and began to unfold it.

"Seriously though, my boy," Clyde said, "I was just asking myself why ol' Pat hadn't been in lately to fondle the guns. Yes indeed. Now, good buddy, I'd be much obliged if you would try out the action on this new thirty-thirty and give me your expert opinion of it."

They Shoot Canoes, Don't They?

☞ ☞ ☞**A** while back my friend Retch Sweeney and I were hiking through a wilderness area and happened to come across these three guys who were pretending to cling to the side of a mountain as if their lives depended on it. They were dressed in funny little costumes and all tied together on a long rope. Their leader was pounding what looked like a big spike into a crack in the rock. We guessed right off what they were up to. They were obviously being initiated into a college fraternity, and this was part of the hazing. Not wishing to embarrass them any more than was absolutely necessary, Retch and I just let on as if everything was normal and that scarcely a day went by that we didn't see people in funny costumes hammering nails into rock.

"We seem to have taken a wrong turn back there a ways," I said to them. "Could you give us some idea where we are?"

The three pledgies seemed both angered and astonished at seeing us. "Why, this is the North Face of Mount

Terrible," the leader said. "We're making an assault on it. You shouldn't be up here!"

"You're telling me!" I said. "We're supposed to be on our way to Wild Rose Lake."

"Say, it's none of my business," Retch put in, "but this thing you're makin', don't you think you would get it built a lot faster if you found some level ground? It's pretty steep up here."

That didn't seem to set too well with them, or at least so I interpreted from their flared nostrils and narrowed eyes.

"Say, don't let a couple of flabby, middle-aged men disturb you," I said. "We'll just mosey on past you and climb up to the top of this hill and get out of your way. Maybe we can get a bearing on Wild Rose Lake from up there."

Well, I was glad they were all roped together and the rope was fastened to one of the spikes they had hammered into the rock. Otherwise, I think they would have taken off after us, and that slope was so steep you could just barely walk on it, let alone run. They would have caught us for sure.

"Those guys certainly weren't too friendly, were they?" Retch said later.

"No, they weren't," I said. "The very least they could have done was offer to give us a hand with the canoe."

Upon later reflection, I came to the conclusion that it was probably the canoe itself that had disturbed the pledgies. There are people who can't get within fifteen feet of a canoe without turning psychotic or, as my psychiatrist puts it, "going bananas."

I've been around canoes most of my life and have high regard for them. They're versatile and efficient and serve the angler and hunter well. But I have no truck with the sentimental nonsense often associated with them. Some years back I wrecked an old canoe of mine that I had spent hundreds of happy hours in. When I saw there was no way to salvage it, I tossed it on top of the car rack and hauled it out to the city dump. That was it. There was no sentimental nonsense involved. Just to show you some of the strange things that can happen, though, a few days later my wife went out to clean the garage and found the canoe back in its old place.

I had to laugh. "Well, I'll be darned," I said. "The old thing must have followed me home from the dump! Well, if it cares that much about me, I guess we'll let it stay."

After babbling sentimentality, the next most prevalent form of irrational behavior evoked by canoes is raw terror (occasionally there is boiled terror or even fried terror, but usually it's raw). Take my neighbor Al Finley, the city councilperson, for example. I figured that anyone so adept at floating bond issues as Finley certainly wouldn't have any trouble floating a canoe—a duck to water, so to speak. I've taught him most of the paddle strokes and he is quite proficient at them, but he has never gotten over his fear of canoes.

"Careful!" he screams. "It's tipping! It's tipping! Watch that rock! Careful!"

The way he acts is absolutely pathetic. I don't know what he'd do if we ever put the canoe in the water.

Some canoe-induced behavior is so odd you can't even put a name to it. Take the time I was canoeing up in Canada with Dork Simp, a chap who had been a staunch atheist for as long as I could remember. When we saw that we had made a mistake and had to shoot the Good God Almighty Rapids (named by the first trapper to take a raft of furs down the river), Dork yelled out that he had recently had some serious doubts about the intellectual validity of atheism.

"Forget philosophy, for pete's sake!" I screamed at him. "It's getting rough! Get off that seat and kneel down in the canoe!"

"Amen to that," he yelled back. "You say the words first and I'll try to follow along!"

We smacked into a rock and broke several ribs, two of which, incidentally, seemed to be mine. As we slid sideways off the rock, Dork shouted out that he had just found religion.

A few seconds later, as we were paddling up out of the vortex of a whirlpool, he swore off smoking, drinking, and profanity, the last of which cut his vocabulary by approximately half. When we were at last forcibly ejected from the lower end of the rapids, Dork said that he had decided to enter the ministry.

"It's been a lifelong ambition of mine," he added.

"What!" I said. "Why, not more than fifteen minutes ago you were an atheist."

"Was it only fifteen minutes?" he said. "I could have sworn it was a lifetime!"

The weirdest reaction to canoes that I've ever observed took place in Kelly's Bar & Grill. I had just walked in and mounted a barstool next to Doc Moos, owner and operator of Doc's Boat Works, where I had Zelda, my old wood-and-canvas canoe, in for repairs. Doc was chatting with a new bartender Kelly had hired, a great dull slab of a man but pleasant enough, or so he seemed at first.

"How's my Zelda doing, Doc?" I asked.

"I got bad news for you," Doc said. "I couldn't save her."

"Oh no!" I moaned. "I can't get along without her."

The bartender gave me a sympathetic look. "Gee, I'm sorry fella," he said. "Here, have a drink on Kelly."

I thanked him brusquely, not wanting him to mistake my concern about Zelda for maudlin sentimentality.

"What went wrong?" I asked Doc.

"Well, first of all, as you know, she was cracked and peeling all over, but that was no real problem since we could have put a new fiberglass skin on her. But . . ."

"You can do that now, can you, Doc, put on a fiberglass skin?" the bartender asked.

"Sure," Doc told him. "It's quite a bit of work and expensive, but it wears forever."

"I bet it does," the bartender said. "But how does it look?"

"Just like new," Doc said. "Paint it a nice glossy red or green and it'll knock your eye out."

The bartender looked astounded. "I would've thought pink," he said.

"Pink!" Doc and I both shuddered. The man was totally without taste.

"Anyway," Doc went on, doing his best to ignore the bartender, "some of her ribs were busted up pretty bad. I was going to work up some new ones out of some oak boards I got in the shop . . ."

"What won't they think of next!" the bartender said. "Wood ribs!"

"But as I was saying," Doc continued, shaking his head, "that was when we found the dry rot."

"Oh no, not dry rot!" I moaned.

"Gee, dry rot," the bartender said. "I think my brother got that once from not washin' between his toes."

"Well, it was fatal for Zelda," Doc said.

"Here, have another drink on Kelly," the bartender said.

Up to this time the bartender had seemed like a decent enough fellow, if only slightly smarter than a grapefruit. Now he started to act a bit weird, particularly after I had said something about how much I enjoyed paddling Zelda, even when she was loaded down with all my camping gear. Then Doc asked me what I wanted to do with Zelda's remains. As I say, I'm not much on sentimentality so I told him just to keep them around the shop and use them for parts.

"It's about time I got myself a new one anyway," I said.

"So much for grief, hunh, fella?" the bartender snarled. "Beat the old thing, make her carry all your campin' junk, and then forget her, just like that!" He snapped his fingers so close to my face I jumped.

"What's with you?" I said. "All along I thought you were a canoeist."

That was when he tossed Doc and me out of the bar.

"Call me a canoeist, will you!" he shouted from the doorway. "Listen, fella, I may not be too smart, but I'm a lot more normal than you!"

I suppose these strange attitudes toward canoes are to be expected of persons who don't establish a meaningful relationship with them early in life. My own association with canoes began at age ten. That was when I built my first one. Even if I do say so myself, it was one of the most beautiful canoes I've ever seen.

I built it in a vacant upstairs bedroom out of some old lumber I found in the hog pen. The lumber was dirty and heavy, and I had great difficulty dragging it through the house and up to the bedroom. Most of the difficulty was caused by my mother and grandmother, who kept making nasty remarks about my character and trying to strike me with blunt objects.

It took me about three weeks to build the canoe. If you've never built a canoe, you probably don't realize that the hardest part is shaping the bow and stern just right. I came up with an ingenious solution to this problem that, if it had caught on, would have revolutionized canoe design. I put square ends on it. There were a couple of other minor modifications that also simplified construction—the bottom and sides were flat! I painted it with some red barn paint as a final touch, and the end result was a sharp-looking canoe. Everyone else in my family thought so, too, except Gram. She said it looked like a coffin for someone's pet boa constrictor. Gram, of course, knew next to nothing about boat design.

The canoe's one drawback was that it weighed just slightly less than a Buick, and since I was the only man in the family, we had to ask the old woodsman Rancid Crabtree to come over and help us carry it out of the house.

As Rancid was walking up the stairs, he sniffed the air and asked, "You been keepin' hogs up here? Smells like . . ."

"Never mind what it smells like," Gram snapped. "Just help us carry that contraption out of the house."

Mom, Gram, and I got at one end of the canoe and Rancid at the other, and with a great deal of shouting and groaning managed to lift it until it was resting on our shoulders. We carried it out of the bedroom to the head of the stairs, at which point Rancid gasped that he couldn't hold up his end a second longer. While he was looking around frantically for something to rest the canoe on, he accidentally stepped down backwards onto the stairs. We at the rear end of the canoe naturally assumed from this gesture that he had changed his mind about resting, so we charged forward. It was just one of those innocent misunderstandings. As it turned out, no one was seriously injured, but some of the language would have made the hair of a wart hog stand on end. The only ill effect I suffered was psychological. As we all galloped around the sharp turn at the landing, I caught a glimpse of the expression on Rancid's face, and it just wasn't the sort of thing a ten-year-old boy should be allowed to see. For years afterwards, it would cause me to wake up whimpering in the night.

When Rancid came into the kitchen for coffee after the ordeal was over, he complained that he felt two feet shorter. Gram pointed out to him that he was walking on his knees. Rancid was always doing comical things like that.

Beautiful as it was, my first canoe was never launched but sat for years in the yard at the place where it was dropped. My mother later filled it with dirt and planted flowers in it. Strangers sometimes got the mistaken impression from it that we were holding a funeral for a tall, thin gangster.

The first store-bought canoe with which I had a meaningful relationship was hidden in some brush on the banks of a creek near where I lived. During the spring of the year, the creek was deep and fast with some nice rapids in it, but I had enough sense to realize that it would be dangerous for me to attempt to paddle the canoe down it. The main reason it would have been dangerous was that the big kid who owned the canoe had threatened to put me in a sack and toss the sack in the creek if he caught me messing around with it.

The big kid's name was Buster, and he divided his time among eating, sleeping, and beating up people, although not necessarily in that order. Sometimes he would catch me down by the creek and practice his beating-up techniques on me. Although these sessions were more monotonous than painful, they were sufficiently instructive to make me realize that I didn't want Buster performing real beating-up on me.

Nevertheless, I could not force myself to stay entirely

away from the canoe, a lovely little fifteen-footer, mostly green but with a patch of white on the side where Buster had attempted to paint over the words PROPERTY OF SUNSET RESORT. Once, I even slipped the canoe into the water just to see how it floated. It floated fine. After giving considerable thought to the questions (1) how much fun would it be to paddle the canoe around a bit, and (2) how difficult would it be to swim while confined in a sack, I slipped the canoe back into its hiding place and wiped off my fingerprints.

About a mile from my home, the creek wound through a swamp that was full of dead trees, rotting stumps, quicksand, mud flats, snakes, frogs, slime—all the usual neat swamp stuff. Brook trout the size of alligators were said to inhabit the deeper waters of the swamp, and I would occasionally pole my log raft into the dark interior in search of them. It was on one of these excursions that I happened to come upon Buster's canoe, bobbing gently among the cattails that surrounded a small, brush-covered island. My heart leaped up.

"Well, I'll be darned!" I said to myself. "Ol' Buster's canoe has somehow slid itself into the crick and drifted into the swamp. Won't he be tickled pink when I bring it back to him—in a day or two or the week after next at the latest?"

My elation, however, was diluted by a sense of foreboding, even though there wasn't a sign of human life in any direction. I eased myself silently into the canoe and set the raft adrift, just in case someone might get the notion of using it as a means of pursuing me.

That the canoe had somehow drifted upstream and tied itself to a branch with a length of clothesline and a square knot were matters of no little curiosity to me, and I remember making a mental note to ask my arithmetic teacher what the odds of such an occurrence might be.

As I was untying the square knot, I happened to glance out from among the cattails. What I saw momentarily freeze-dried my corpuscles. Strolling right toward me, arm-in-arm from out of the brush in the middle of the island, were Buster and a girl by the name of Alvira Holstein. Even as it was locked in the grip of terror, my fertile mind groped with the question of what the two of them could be doing on the island, Buster never having struck me as much of a picnicker. On the other hand, the occasion didn't seem appropriate for casual conversation. I did take some comfort in the fact that Buster did not appear to have a sack with him.

Upon seeing me crouched in his canoe, Buster let out a roar that is best described as approximating that of a grizzly bear having a bicuspid extracted without benefit of anesthetic. I had never paddled a canoe before, but at that instant, such was the inspiration of seeing Buster charging toward me, I instantly discovered that I had a talent for it bordering on genius. Within seconds I had the canoe moving at sufficient momentum to plane easily over half-submerged logs, mud flats, and flocks of waterfowl caught unawares. I looked back once, and Buster was still in hot pursuit, even though he was up to his armpits in swamp slime. He was screeching almost incoherently, something to the effect that he would make sweeping but imaginative alterations on my anatomy once he laid hands on it. Alvira Holstein was jumping up and down on the island, crying and screaming, and yelling out, "Don't kill him, Buster, don't kill him!" Even to this day it sets my nerves on edge to hear a woman yell something like that.

I paddled the canoe halfway to my house, which was remarkable only in that the water ended some distance short of that. My grandmother was in the kitchen when I burst through the door.

"Land sakes, what's after you?" she said.

"Never mind that now," I said. "Just tell me this. Is there really quicksand in the swamp?"

"There certainly is," she said. "And you just stay out of that swamp if you don't want to get swallowed up by it!"

I crossed my fingers. "Come on, *quicksand!*" I said.

Actually, it was Gram who finally saved me from the sack or, at best, going through life as a very odd-looking person. When she found out Buster was after me, she just scoffed.

"Buster ain't going to hurt you," she said, neglecting to mention why I should be an exception to the rule. "If he does, you just tell the sheriff on him. The sheriff's a tough man, and he don't stand for no nonsense."

"Yeah, he's tough all right," I said, pulling back the window curtain an inch to peer out. "But he don't bother about kids' fightin'. He says it's just natural."

"Oh, I don't know," Gram said. "Sheriff Holstein's a pretty sensible man, and I think if you just told him . . ."

"Holstein?" I said. "That's right, it *is* Sheriff Holstein, isn't it?" I walked away from the window, cut myself a slab of fresh-baked bread, and smeared on a layer of raspberry jam.

"Well, forget about Buster, Gram," I told her. "I got to go paddle my canoe."

My First Deer,
and Welcome to It

☞ ☞ ☞ **F**or a first deer, there is no habitat so lush and fine as a hunter's memory Three decades and more of observation have convinced me that a first deer not only lives on in the memory of a hunter but thrives there, increasing in points and pounds with each passing year until at last it reaches full maturity, which is to say, big enough to shade a team of Belgian draft horses in its shadow at high noon. It is a remarkable phenomenon and worthy of study.

Consider the case of my friend Retch Sweeney and his first deer. I was with him when he shot the deer, and though my first impression was that Retch had killed a large jackrabbit, closer examination revealed it to be a little spike buck. We were both only fourteen at the time and quivering with excitement over Retch's good fortune in getting his first deer. Still, there was no question in either of our minds that what he had bagged was a spike buck, one slightly larger than a bread box.

You can imagine my surprise when, scarcely a month later, I overheard Retch telling some friends that his first

deer was a nice four-point buck. I mentioned to Retch
afterwards that I was amazed at how fast his deer was
growing. He said he was a little surprised himself but was
pleased it was doing so well. He admitted that he had
known all along that the deer was going to get bigger
eventually although he hadn't expected it to happen so
quickly. Staring off into the middle distance, a dreamy
expression on his face, he told me, "You know, I wouldn't
be surprised if someday my first deer becomes a world's-
record trophy."

"I wouldn't either," I said. "In fact, I'd be willing to
bet on it."

Not long ago, Retch and I were chatting with some of
the boys down at Kelly's Bar & Grill and the talk turned
to first deer. It was disgusting. I can stand maudlin
sentimentality as well as the next fellow, but I have my
limits. Some of those first deer had a mastery of escape
routines that would have put Houdini to shame. Most of
them were so smart there was some question in my mind
as to whether the hunter had bagged a deer or a Rhodes
Scholar. I wanted to ask them if they had tagged their
buck or awarded it a Phi Beta Kappa key. And big! There
wasn't a deer there who couldn't have cradled a baby
grand piano in its rack. Finally it was Retch's turn, and
between waves of nausea I wondered whether that little
spike buck had developed enough over the years to meet
this kind of competition. I needn't have wondered.

Retch's deer no longer walked in typical deer fashion; it "ghosted" about through the trees like an appari-
tion. When it galloped, though, the sound was "like
thunder rolling through the hills." And so help me, "fire
flickered in its eyes." Its tracks "looked like they'd been
excavated with a backhoe, they were that big." Smart?
That deer could have taught field tactics at West Point.
Retch's little spike buck had come a long way, baby.

At last Retch reached the climax of his story. "I don't expect you boys to believe this," he said, his voice hushed with reverence, "but when I dropped that deer, the mountain *trembled!*"

The boys all nodded, believing. Why, hadn't the mountain trembled for them too when they shot their first deer? Of course it had. All first deer are like that.

Except mine.

I banged the table for attention. "Now," I said, "I'm going to tell you about a *real* first deer, not a figment of my senility, not some fossilized hope of my gangling adolescence, but a *real* first deer."

Now I could tell from looking at their stunned faces that the boys were upset. There is nothing that angers the participants of a bull session more than someone who refuses to engage in the mutual exchange of illusions, someone who tells the simple truth, unstretched, unvarnished, unembellished, and whole.

"Even though it violates the code of the true sportsperson," I began, "I must confess that I still harbor unkind thoughts for my first deer. True to his form and unlike almost all other first deer, he has steadfastly refused to grow in either my memory or imagination; he simply stands there in original size and puny rack, peering over the lip of my consciousness, an insolent smirk decorating his pointy face. Here I offered that thankless creature escape from the anonymity of becoming someone else's second or seventh or seventeenth deer or, at the very least, from an old age presided over by coyotes. And how did he repay me? With humiliation!"

The boys at Kelly's shrank back in horror at this heresy. Retch Sweeney tried to slip away, but I riveted him to his chair with a maniacal laugh. His eyes pleaded with me. "*No, don't tell us!*" they said. "*Don't destroy the myth*

of the first deer!" (which is a pretty long speech for a couple
of beady, bloodshot eyes).

Unrelenting and with only an occasional pause for a
bitter, sardonic cackle to escape my foam-flecked lips, I
plunged on with the tale, stripping away layer after layer
of myth until at last the truth about one man's first deer
had been disrobed and lay before them in all its grim and
naked majesty, shivering and covered with goose bumps.

I began by pointing out what I considered to be one
of the great bureaucratic absurdities of all time: that a
boy at age fourteen was allowed to purchase his first
hunting license and deer tag but was prevented from
obtaining a driver's license until he was sixteen. This was
like telling a kid he could go swimming but to stay away
from the water. Did the bureaucrats think that trophy
mule deer came down from the hills in the evening to
drink out of your garden hose? The predicament left you
no recourse but to beg the adult hunters you knew to take
you hunting with them on weekends. My problem was
that all the adult hunters I knew bagged their deer in the
first couple of weeks of the season, and from then on I
had to furnish my own transportation. This meant that in
order to get up to the top of the mountain where the
trophy mule deer hung out, I had to start out at four in
the morning if I wanted to be there by noon. I remember
one time when I was steering around some big boulders
in the road about three-quarters of the way up the
Dawson Grade and a Jeep with two hunters in it came
plowing up behind me. I pulled over so they could pass.
The hunters grinned at me as they went by. You'd think
they'd never before seen anyone pedaling a bike twenty
miles up the side of a mountain to go deer hunting.

I had rigged up my bike especially for deer hunting.
There were straps to hold my rifle snugly across the
handlebars, and saddlebags draped over the back fender

to carry my gear. The back fender had been reinforced to support a sturdy platform, my reason for this being that I didn't believe the original fender was stout enough to support a buck when I got one. My one oversight was failing to put a guard over the top of the bike chain, in which I had to worry constantly about getting my tongue caught. Deer hunting on a bike was no picnic.

A mile farther on and a couple of hours later I came to where the fellows in the Jeep were busy setting up camp with some other hunters. Apparently, someone told a fantastic joke just as I went pumping by because they all collapsed in a fit of laughter and were doubled over and rolling on the ground and pounding trees with their fists. They seemed like a bunch of lunatics to me, and I hoped they didn't plan on hunting in the same area I was headed for. I couldn't wait to see their faces when I came coasting easily back down the mountain with a trophy buck draped over the back of my bike.

One of the main problems with biking your way out to hunt deer was that, if you left at four in the morning, by the time you got to the hunting place there were only a couple of hours of daylight left in which to do your hunting. Then you had to spend some time resting, at least until the pounding of your heart eased up enough not to frighten the deer.

As luck would have it, just as I was unstrapping my rifle from the handlebars, a buck mule deer came dancing out of the brush not twenty yards away from me. Now right then I should have known he was up to no good. He had doubtless been lying on a ledge and watching me for hours as I pumped my way up the mountain. He had probably even snickered to himself as he plotted ways to embarrass me.

All the time I was easing the rifle loose from the handlebars, digging a shell out of my pocket, and thumbing it into the rifle, the deer danced and clowned and cut up all around me, smirking the whole while. The instant I jacked the shell into the chamber, however, he stepped behind a tree. I darted to one side, rifle at the ready. He moved to the other side of the tree and stuck his head out just enough so I could see him feigning a yawn. As I moved up close to the tree, he did a rapid tiptoe to another tree. I heard him snort with laughter. For a whole hour he toyed with me in this manner, enjoying himself immensely. Then I fooled him, or at least so I thought at the time. I turned and started walking in a dejected manner back toward my bike, still watching his hiding place out of the corner of my eye. He stuck his head out to see what I was up to. I stepped behind a small bush and knelt as if to tie my shoe. Then, swiftly I turned, drew a bead on his head, and fired. Down he went.

I was still congratulating myself on a fine shot when I rushed up to his crumpled form. Strangely, I could not detect a bullet hole in his head, but one of his antlers was chipped and I figured the slug had struck there with sufficient force to do him in. "No matter," I said to myself, "I have at last got my first deer," and I pictured in my mind the joyous welcome I would receive when I came home hauling in a hundred or so pounds of venison. Then I discovered my knife had fallen out of its sheath during my frantic pursuit of the deer. Instant anguish! The question that nagged my waking moments for years afterwards was: Did the deer know that I had dropped my knife? Had I only interpreted it correctly, the answer to that question was written all over the buck's face—he was still wearing that stupid smirk.

"Well," I told myself, "what I'll do is just load him on my bike, haul him down to the lunatic hunters' camp, and borrow a knife from them to dress him out with." I

thought this plan particularly good in that it would offer
me the opportunity to give those smart alecks a few tips
on deer hunting.

Loading the buck on the bike was much more of a
problem than I had expected. When I draped him
crosswise over the platform on the rear fender, his head
and front quarters dragged on one side and his rear
quarters on the other. Several times as I lifted and pulled
and hauled, I thought I heard a giggle, but when I
looked around nobody was there. It was during one of
these pauses that a brilliant idea occurred to me. With
herculean effort, I managed to arrange the deer so that
he was sitting astraddle of the platform, his four legs
splayed out forward and his head drooping down. I
lashed his front feet to the handlebars, one on each side.
Then I slid up onto the seat ahead of him, draped his
head over my right shoulder, and pushed off.

I must admit that riding a bike with a deer on behind
was a good deal more difficult than I had anticipated.
Even though I pressed down on the brake for all I was
worth, our wobbling descent was much faster than I
would have liked. The road was narrow, twisting, and
filled with ruts and large rocks, with breathtaking drop-
offs on the outer edge. When we came hurtling around a
sharp, high bend above the hunters' camp, I glanced
down. Even from that distance I could see their eyes pop
and their jaws sag as they caught sight of us.

What worried me most was the hill that led down to
the camp. As we arrived at the crest of it, my heart, liver,
and kidneys all jumped in unison. The hill was much
steeper than I had remembered. It was at that point that
the buck gave a loud, startled snort.

My first deer had either just regained consciousness
or been shocked out of his pretense of death at the sight
of the plummeting grade before us. We both tried to leap

free of the bike, but he was tied on and I was locked in the embrace of his front legs.

When we shot past the hunters' camp, I was too occupied at the moment to get a good look at their faces. I heard afterwards that a game warden found them several hours later, frozen in various postures and still staring at the road in front of their camp. The report was probably exaggerated, however, game wardens being little better than hunters at sticking to the simple truth.

I probably would have been able to get the bike stopped sooner and with fewer injuries to myself if I had had enough sense to tie down the deer's hind legs. As it was, he started flailing wildly about with them and somehow managed to get his hooves on the pedals. By the time we reached the bottom of the mountain he not only had the hang of pedaling but was showing consider-able talent for it. He also seemed to be enjoying himself immensely. We zoomed up and down over the rolling foothills and into the bottomlands, with the deer pedal-ing wildly and me shouting and cursing and trying to wrest control of the bike from him. At last he piled us up in the middle of a farmer's pumpkin patch. He tore himself loose from the bike and bounded into the woods, all the while making obscene gestures at me with his tail. I threw the rifle to my shoulder and got off one quick shot. It might have hit him too, if the bike hadn't been still strapped to the rifle.

"Now that," I said to the boys at Kelly's, "is how to tell about a first deer—a straightforward factual report unadorned by a lot of lies and sentimentality."

Unrepentant, they muttered angrily. To soothe their injured feelings, I told them about my second deer. It was so big it could cradle a baby grand piano in its rack and shade a team of Belgian draft horses in its shadow at high noon. Honest! I wouldn't lie about a thing like that.

The Crouch Hop
and Other Useful
Outdoor Steps

☞ ☞ ☞ **W**hile going through my mail at breakfast the other morning, I noticed a picture on a magazine cover of what was purported to be a group of backpackers. The individuals portrayed were all neat, clean, and beaming with happy smiles as they came striding up over a grassy knoll.

"Those aren't backpackers, they're fashion models," I told my wife.

Always keen to assimilate my wisdom on such matters, she fixed me with an intense look. "Did you eat my piece of bacon? That last piece of bacon was *mine!*"

"Well, first of all," I explained patiently, "they're all neat, clean, and beaming with happy smiles, whereas backpackers are generally messy, grubby, and grunting. Second, they're climbing a grassy knoll instead of a forty-five-degree, rock-strewn snake path the Forest Service laughingly calls a trail. What really gives them away, though, is that they're *striding*. No self-respecting backpacker would be caught dead striding."

"You even ate my English muffin!" my wife shouted.

This enlightening exchange got me to thinking that there are probably many people like my wife who have waited in vain for someone to erase their ignorance concerning the various foot movements, or steps, as they are sometimes called, employed in the practice of outdoor sports. I herewith offer as a public service the following compendium of the basic forms of outdoor pedestrianism.

THE PACKER'S PLOD—Backpackers, being generally optimistic souls, will start off on an excursion at a brisk pace, which they maintain for approximately nine steps. They then shift into the standard packer's plod. One foot is raised and placed forward three inches on the trail. The backpacker then breathes deeply, checks his hip strap, wipes the perspiration off his face, takes a swig from his canteen, eats a piece of beef jerky, snaps a photograph of a Stellar's jay, and consults his map. Then he repeats the process. A good backpacker, if he had a table handy, could play a hand of solitaire between steps. His forward motion defies detection by the human eye. Nevertheless, his progress is steady and unrelenting, and during the course of a day he can eat up a surprising number of miles, not to mention several pounds of jerky.

It always amuses experienced backpackers to see neophytes of the sport go racing past them on the trail. The tale of the tortoise and the hare leaps instantly to mind. Last summer my old backpacking partner Vern Schulze and I took his two boys, Wayne and Jim, on their first overnight hike. Our destination was a lake high up in the mountains of Idaho. Vern and I set off at the standard packer's plod, while the boys tore off up the trail ahead of us, soon disappearing from view. After about an hour they came racing back down the trail.

"What happened?" they shouted. "When you didn't show up at the lake, we thought maybe you had fallen and hurt yourselves."

Vern and I just winked at each other. "Don't worry about us. You fellows just go on ahead. We'll catch up."

After the boys had charged back up the trail, I said to Vern, "You know, when Wayne and Jim are exhausted and we pass them up, it would be better if we didn't tease them too much. It's a bad thing to break a boy's spirit."

"Right," Vern said, munching a handful of beef jerky while he snapped a picture of a Stellar's jay.

A couple of hours later the boys came jogging back down the trail.

"Look," I whispered to Vern. "They're already starting to slow down."

"Hey, Dad!" Wayne shouted. "The fish are really biting great! We've already caught enough for supper!"

It was all we could do to suppress our mirth. Both youngsters were showing definite signs of burning themselves out.

"You guys better speed it up a bit," Jim said.

"We can take care of ourselves," Vern replied, giving me a nudge with his elbow that almost toppled me off the trail. "Say, if you guys want to sit down and take a rest, go right ahead. It's nothing to be ashamed of. Just because Pat and I never stop doesn't mean you shouldn't."

"I thought you were stopped right now," Jim said.

"No," Vern said, "as a matter of fact we have just quickened our pace."

"We'd better be going," Wayne said. "We've got the tent pitched and a rock fireplace made and want to finish gathering wood for the fire."

They made three or four more trips back to check on us, each time moving a little slower. Along about evening we came upon them sitting alongside the trail eating

huckleberries, and they both looked plumb tuckered out.
Vern and I passed them up without so much as a single
unkind remark. When we had dumped our packs in
camp, though, I couldn't help offering a bit of advice to
Wayne, who was hunkered at my feet.

"Easy does it," I told him. "If you pull a man's boots
off too fast it hurts his ankles."

A boy is never too young to start learning the basics
of backpacking, I always say.

THE SIDEWINDER—Skilled anglers the world over are
masters of this rather peculiar outdoor step. Essentially,
it consists of sauntering sideways. While looking straight
ahead as if wearing blinders, you attempt to give the
impression that you are oblivious to what is taking place
on either side of you. The situation in which it is used is
this: Your partner has laid claim to a nice piece of fishing
water twenty yards or so downstream from you. Suddenly he gets a strike and flicks his fly into the uppermost
branches of a thorn apple. You know the fish was a big
one because of the way your friend suddenly crouches
down and scurries about like a hyperactive crab as he
tries to untangle his line and stay out of sight of the fish at
the same time. There is a great temptation on such
occasions to be overwhelmed by your partner's desperate
maneuvers and to laugh yourself senseless. A master
angler, however, will maintain an expression that is not
only sober but that conveys the impression he is totally
unaware of anything but his own rhythmic casting. While
maintaining this expression, he then performs the sidewinder, which carries him sideways along the bank to that
portion of water where the monster trout has signaled its
presence. Upon arriving at this position, the master
angler must make a pretense of being in a trance of
sufficient depth that it cannot be penetrated by the vile
epithets screamed at him by his former friend. The

former friend will at this point give up all caution and throw himself into all-out combat with the thorn apple in order to free the offending line. Catching and landing a fish under such trying circumstances is what qualifies one as a master angler, sometimes referred to by fishing partners as a "no-good *bleep* of a *bleep*." Good sportsmanship requires that one refrain from maniacal laughter after performing a successful sidewinder.

THE MOSEY—This is a walk that belongs almost exclusively to game wardens, and they reserve it for occasions when they are moving in to make a pinch. If you see a man moseying toward you while you are fishing or hunting, you had better make a quick study of your game regulations because you may be in trouble. If game wardens in your area are prone to being sneaky, a stump or a bush moseying toward you also may mean trouble. I myself have on occasion put the mosey to good use. Indeed, it is rather amusing to see how quickly other anglers can be cleared from a stream by the simple expedient of moseying toward them.

THE HEEL-AND-TOE—This is essentially the same step employed in the track event of the same name. It is characterized by quick, tiny steps, an exaggeratedly straight vertical posture, and a facial expression combined of equal parts of indignation and suffering. It is not unusual to see a whole party of elk hunters going about camp in this fashion after a twenty-mile horseback ride into the mountains.

THE CROUCH HOP—This is usually performed midway through the process of driving in a tent peg with a large flat rock. The individual will suddenly leap up, clamp one of his hands between his thighs, and, making strange grunting sounds, begin to hop madly about the camp. I have performed this exercise many times, and it does wonders for relieving the pain resulting from a finger caught between a rock and a tent peg. It is equally important to recognize the crouch hop for what it is when you see it being performed. Once in Yellowstone Park, blinded by tears, I accidentally crouch-hopped into the adjoining camp space where an hysterical lady tried to run me through with her wiener stick. Luckily for me, she didn't have sufficient foresight to remove the wiener and I escaped with a single bruise no larger than the business end of a Ball Park frank.

THE SAUNTER—The saunter is applicable almost exclusively to bird hunting. I can remember the very first time I used it. I was fourteen and grouse hunting with my friend Retch Sweeney. We were moving stealthily through a thick stand of evergreens where we knew a grouse to be hiding. Suddenly the bird exploded off a limb almost directly above us and roared away through the trees. Startled, I whirled, pointed my old double-barrel at a patch of sky as big around as a bread box, and fired. Out of sheer coincidence, the shot and the grouse arrived at that patch of sky simultaneously, and the bird landed with a dead thump ten yards away. All my instincts told me to race over, grab up the grouse, and clamp it to my throbbing chest, all the while exclaiming, "Holy cow! Did you see that shot? Holy cow! What a shot!" For the first time in my life, however, I defied my instincts. I s-a-u-n-t-e-r-e-d over, picked up the grouse, and nonchalantly deposited it in my game pocket. "That one sort of surprised me," I said to Retch, whose tongue still dangled limply from his gaping mouth.

Now, had I gone bounding and bawling after that grouse like a hound pup after a squirrel, Retch would have known the shot was an accident. Instead, my saunter filled the great empty spaces of his mind with the impression that I was a fantastic wing shot. He frequently commented afterwards that he didn't understand how anyone who was such a great shot could miss so often. I have found, in fact, that a properly executed saunter after downed game will sustain one's reputation as a great shot through an unbroken string of twenty-five misses.

If one hunts with a dog, by the way, the same effect can be achieved by teaching it to retrieve game in a manner that suggests unrelieved boredom. Personally, I haven't had much success in this area with my own dog, since I've never been able to break him of the habit of doing a histrionic double take every time I hit something. You just can't compensate for bad breeding, so there is nothing for me to do but saunter to make up for a stupid dog who aspires to be a stand-up comic.

THE TRUDGE—Used primarily for returning to one's car after a cold, wet, windy day of hunting and you missed three easy shots and it's the last day of the season and you can't remember where you left your car.

THE LOPE—Basically a fast saunter, in that it implies casualness. Say you're out fishing a remote mountain stream with your boy and along toward dusk the hair on the back of your neck, for no reason at all, rises. You have the distinct impression that you are being *watched*. You halt a cast in mid-air and reel in.

"What you doin'?" the boy says. "I just had a good bite."

"It's getting late," you say. "We'd better head home." You then take off at a lope.

"Well, shoot!" the boy says.

THE SHAMBLE—What the boy does in the above situation.

THE BOLT—What the lope is changed into if the feeling of being watched is followed by a low, rumbling growl and a crashing in the brush. Actually, a low, rumbling growl or a crashing in the brush are sufficient reasons in themselves to engage in a bolt.

THE TRAMPLE—What the boy does to you when he hears the low, rumbling growl and crashing in the brush.

There are literally dozens of other interesting and enjoyable outdoor steps, but those given above are basic. It might be well to practice them at home until you feel both comfortable and confident with them. As a matter of fact, my wife just crouch-hopped past the door of my study. I wonder what she was doing driving a tent peg with a flat rock when she was supposed to be hanging a picture.

Meanwhile,
Back at the
B Western

☞ ☞ ☞**F**ew people appreciate the great contribution the handgun has made to television and motion pictures. What would police shows, for example, be without .38 Specials and .357 Magnums? Imagine police detectives standing around the squad room in shirtsleeves, rifles dangling from under their armpits. Ridiculous!

The shows that would really suffer from an absence of handguns, though, would be the westerns. Without the pistol, there would be no fast draw, and without the fast draw, westerns would be a whole lot different. Consider, if you will, and if you have the stomach for it, a quick-draw scene with rifles. Matt Dillon clumps out into the street from the Long Branch Saloon to issue a warning to one of the quaintly named villains so characteristic of "Gunsmoke."

"Chester and I caught you red-handed stealin' buffalo humps up on the flat, Ick Crud," he says. "You be outta town by sundown if you know what's good fer ya. Folks here 'bouts don't take kindly to buffalo-humpers."

Ick Crud sneers. "Reach fer yer iron, Marshal!"

The camera zooms in for a close-up of Matt's low-slung Winchester, the tie-downs knotted around his ankle. Quicker than Dean Martin can sing "Old Man River," Matt draws . . . and draws . . . and draws. Ick Crud uses a frantic hand-over-hand draw on his Sharps-Borchardt. During the draw, Chester, Doc, and Miss Kitty go back into the Long Branch for a drink to steady their nerves.

"Three whiskeys and be quick about it," Miss Kitty snaps to the bartender. "Matt's drawin' out there in the street, and we ain't got much time before the shootin' starts."

"I don't know why Matt don't git outta the marshaling business," Doc grumbles. "I keep tellin' him, 'Matt, sooner or later a gunfighter's gonna shade your draw by just a minute or two, and that'll be it fer ya.'"

"We better git back out there," Chester whines. "They should be just about finished drawin', and I don't want to miss the shootin'."

No doubt about it, the handgun and the fast draw are essential to the true western, and any movie fan worth his hot-buttered popcorn not only expects them to be in the western but knows the ritual by heart. The ritual usually begins with the "call out." The villain stands in the street and calls out the hero—"C'mon out, Ringo, you yellow-bellied, chicken-livered, varicose-veined, spastic-coloned wimp!"

Upon hearing himself being called out, the hero immediately begins his preparations. He tosses down his shot of whiskey and grinds out his cigar on the greasy nose of the belligerent bartender. He slips his pistol out of its holster and checks the cylinder to make sure he reloaded after his last shoot-out. (There is nothing more disappointing than to beat the other fellow to the draw and then discover that you forgot to reload.) He then reholsters his gun and slips it out and in a few times to make sure it isn't sticking. (A stuck gun is just about as bad as an unloaded one.) Next he unstraps his spurs, his motive here apparently being that, should he change his mind about the fight, it is a lot easier to run when you're not wearing spurs. He pulls his hat low over his eyes, limbers up the fingers of his gun hand, and tucks his jacket back behind the butt of his revolver. One purpose of all this preparation may be the hope that the villain will get tired of waiting and go home. The villain never does, of course, although sometimes he gets a cramp in his lip from holding a sneer so long.

Back in the olden days when I was a kid, we had what were called the B westerns. The B stood for "best." These were movies starring Roy Rogers, Gene Autry, and Hopalong Cassidy. They weren't anything like the westerns nowadays starring Clint Eastwood, the ones where you have to buy a program to tell the good guys from the bad guys. In the B westerns, you always knew the good guys. They were neatly dressed, clean-shaven, and didn't cuss, smoke, drink, kiss, or do anything else that was bad for health or morals. Even the bad guys didn't do most of these things, but you could tell them anyway. For one thing, they all used the interrupted curse:

"What the . . . !"
"Well, I'll be . . . !"
"Why you . . . !"

They had real action in the B's too, not like the "modern" western where you spend half the movie watching Eastwood squint his eyes and ripple his jaw muscles. Clint holsters his gun like he was setting a carton of milk back in a refrigerator. Why, Roy, Gene, and Hoppy wouldn't even think of putting their guns back into their holsters without giving them a twirl or two first.

I don't recall seeing Roy, Gene, or Hoppy ever shoot anybody, but they probably did. Usually, they just shot the gun out of the villain's hand and let it go at that. Sometimes they would rope the bad guys, often getting a single loop of their lasso around the whole gang. Heroes knew their business in the B westerns.

One nice bit of business Roy, Gene, and Hoppy perfected was to leapfrog over the rumps of their horses and land smack in the saddle. They never landed on the saddle horn either, although once I think I heard the Lone Ranger cry out in a shrill voice, "Hii *owwww* Silver away!"

My cousin Buck, who was several years older than I and knew everything, told me he was an expert at getting on horses like that and that there really wasn't anything to it. I said I couldn't believe that. He said if I had a horse handy he would show me. I said I didn't have a horse but I had a cow. Would a cow work? He said sure. We went out to the pasture and found a cow engaged in licking a salt block. Buck said that one would do just fine. I suggested that we warn the cow of what to expect, but Buck said that wouldn't be necessary. As it turned out, Buck was wrong about that and the rest as well. I still think the cow probably would have cooperated and even entered into the spirit of the thing had we just let her know what to expect. As it was, Buck got back twenty yards or so and made a dash for her. At the exact instant he got his hands on the cow's rump and his legs had crossed over his arms in mid-vault, the cow let out a frightened bellow and bolted forward. As the cow disappeared over a nearby hill, Buck was still perched on her tail bones in a strange variation of the lotus position and screaming, "Whoa, you stupid cow, whoa!"

"Well, I'll be . . . !" I said.

The B western heroes were big on tricks. Say the

villain got the drop on Roy in a little cabin out in the
middle of the desert. Just as the baddy was about to plug
him, Roy would shout "Watch out!" and point over the
other man's shoulder. The villain would spin around,
and Roy would jump him and thump his head to a
fare-thee-well. These villains were *dumb!* Otherwise, why
would they expect the guy they were about to gun down
to warn them of a surprise attack? They were slow to
learn. Roy, Gene, and Hoppy would catch them with this
little trick movie after movie. Maybe the reason they were
so dumb was from getting their heads thumped so often.

Eventually, however, they did start catching on to
the trick. "You ain't foolin' me with that old trick,
Rogers," the bad guy would say, as if he had seen some of
these movies before himself. But this time Gabby Hayes
would actually be sneaking up behind him and would
thump his head a good one. Again, one might wonder
why Roy thought it necessary to warn the villain when his
comical sidekick was in fact sneaking up behind the man.
The reason, of course, was to complicate matters for the
villain when this particular situation arose in future
movies. Roy, Gene, and Hoppy all worked half a dozen
different ploys of this same routine, always with success.
After a while the villain could scarcely get the drop on
one of them without instantly becoming a nervous wreck
from wondering whether or not he was about to be
jumped.

The B western villain was a sucker for pebbles, too.
Anytime the hero wanted to draw the baddy's attention
away from himself, he would toss a pebble. The villain
would whirl around and empty his six-gun into the
pebble. Then he would see that it was only a pebble and
would get this worried, expectant look in his eyes, which
said, "*Head, get ready for a thumping!*"

Counting shots was a favorite tactic of B western

heroes. They would wave a hat around on a stick or perform some other trick to draw fire, all the time counting shots. Then, suddenly, they would walk right out in the open and announce, "Six! That was your last bullet, Slade!" Villains liked to try this trick too, but having the IQ's of celery, they could never get it straight. There was scarcely a villain in B westerns who could count to six without making a mistake. "Six," the bad guy would say, walking out from behind his rock. "That was your last bullet, Autry!"

BANG!

If the movie patron wondered what it was the villain was muttering as he lay sprawled in the dust, it was probably, "Let's see now, two shots ricocheted off the rock, two went through my hat on the stick, that makes five . . ."

Even among the B western audiences there were those who counted shots. They counted the number of shots the hero fired without reloading. I hated these wise guys. Right in the tense part of the movie, they would guffaw: "That's nine shots without reloading! Roy must be using a nine-shooter!"

"Why you . . . !" I would say under my breath. If there was anyone who couldn't appreciate a B western, it was a nitpicker.

The last B western I ever saw in a theater was in a small college town in Idaho. It starred Randolph Scott, and in the big scene the baddies had ganged up on Randolph in the saloon. When they started blazing away at him, Randolph jumped behind a cast-iron stove and, if I recall correctly, used the stove lid as a sort of shield while he returned their fire. The theater was filled with college kids and, as is the nature of college kids, they began whooping and jeering and laughing at Randolph's plight. Seated just behind me were an old farmer and his wife who had paid their hard-earned $1.50 for an evening of serious entertainment. As the slugs were spanging off the stove like lead hail and the college kids were whooping it up, I heard the old woman whisper nervously to her husband. The farmer, in a gruff but gentle voice, reassured her. "Don't worry, Mother," he said, "Ol' Randolph, he'll figure a way to git hisself out of this mess."

You bet! The farmer and his wife were my kind of people.

Looking back, I now realize it was a good thing Hollywood stopped turning out B westerns when it did. I was grown up and had a job by then, and folks were beginning to ask, "What's that big fellow doing down there, sitting in the front row with the kids?"

The Education of a Sportsman

☞ ☞ ☞The letter came in the spring of my eighteenth year, telling me when to report in, and later that summer I packed my few belongings in my rucksack and an old battered suitcase and prepared to depart my home in the mountains of Idaho. Little did I know what lay in store for me during the months ahead, but my mother and grandmother offered plenty of warnings.

"Don't try to be a hero," Gram said.

"You don't have to worry about that," I consoled her.

"I know," Gram said, "but in the off chance the urge comes over you, don't try to be one."

"Right," I said.

"Those people are savages, many of them," Mom said. "They're not like us. I remember the atrocities your father used to tell about when he was in . . ." Her voice trailed off.

"I can't believe it's that bad," I said. "Lonny Henderson went, didn't he, and he came back okay."

Mom shook her head. "No, there's something wrong

with Lonny. Folks say he talks strange now. I don't want that to happen to you."

"Look, don't worry," I said. "I'm going to come back all right. After all, it's not as if I'm going off to war. College is different than that."

Mom and Gram helped me with my packing, and there was considerable discussion over what a young college man should take or leave behind.

"Let's see now," Mom said, surveying my assembled belongings. "You have your fishing rods, your tackle box, your twenty-two, your thirty-thirty, your shotgun, your hunting knife, your hunting boots and wool socks, your lucky hunting hat, your good pair of pants, and your good shirt. Since you're going to be gone for almost a whole year, do you think you might need a change of underwear?"

"Wouldn't hurt," I said. "Why don't you throw in a set?"

"How about the dictionary?" Gram asked.

"Naw," I said. "It'd take up the space of at least four boxes of shells. I know most words, anyway."

"Of course you couldn't think about leaving behind these hides you tanned and the deer head you mounted yourself," Mom added.

"Yeah, I thought my dorm room might need a little decoration, something to make me feel at home." I did wonder a bit about the head, since it had turned out with this stupid grin on its face.

Gram pointed to the big tangle of rusty traps. "You think you might actually have time to run a trap line between classes and studying?"

"There's lots of streams and wild country near the college," I said. "And muskrat hides are probably going to get up to near three dollars this winter."

"Why didn't I think of that?" Gram said.

As it turned out, college was not nearly so dangerous as Gram and Mom had led me to believe. The campus was located in the middle of a vast farming region bordered on one side by a fairly decent range of mountains. The surrounding countryside was dotted with lakes and laced with streams ranging from rivers to creeks to cricks with an occasional swamp thrown in for good luck. From my dorm window, pheasants could be seen strutting the wheat fields and deer were abundant in the mountains. It was my kind of place.

Originally an agricultural school, the college now enjoyed a reputation for research and scholarship in dozens of different academic areas. The chairman of my major department was himself a scholar of international reputation, to which was added the honor of having me as one of his advisees. Later in my college career, after I knew him better, Dr. Osgood revealed to me the peculiar circumstance under which he became my faculty adviser, once and for all clearing up the mystery of how great universities arrive at decisions that will forever influence the future life of a student. "I drew the short straw," he said.

Even now I remember our first meeting. A secretary showed me into an office, where Dr. Osgood, his great mop of white hair seemingly suspended in mid-explosion, sat staring intently at a file folder on his desk. He looked up, smiling.

"From a brief study of your academic record, young man, I see a great future ahead of you as a scholar."

"Gosh," I replied, hanging my head and digging at the carpet with my toe. "I don't know about that."

"Now now now," Dr. Osgood said. "You have amassed a wonderful academic record and are obviously a brilliant student. There's no need for false modesty, Heinzburger."

"McManus," I corrected.

"Oh, *McManus?"* Dr. Osgood picked up another file folder and perused it, occasionally allowing himself a slight shudder. *"Harumph!* Well, now, perhaps I spoke too soon, McManus. It appears from your record that you have every reason for legitimate modesty."

I laughed, not wishing to embarrass him, even though I didn't find his little joke particularly funny.

"By the way, McManus, what happened to the top of your head there, an auto accident?"

"That's my lucky hunting hat, sir."

"Oh. Is it removable or permanently attached?"

"I almost always take it off when I go to bed," I said. "Unless I happen to forget."

"That's most admirable," he said. "One must always strive to cultivate the little niceties." As far as I know, that was the first and only compliment I ever received from Dr. Osgood.

Then we got down to a serious discussion of my academic career, during which Dr. Osgood at times raved incoherently and at other times appeared on the verge of physical violence. Finally, he sat up very straight in his chair and began to perform what I later learned were deep-breathing exercises. Afterwards, for a while, he seemed calmer.

"Let's take a different tack," he said, forcing a small smile that trembled at the corners. "Let's concentrate for a moment on your future, presuming you have one. Now think about this very carefully. All other things aside, what is your ultimate goal in life? When you're as old as I, what single achievement would you like to look back upon, the one great shining accomplishment?"

I could see that we had now got down to serious business, and I sorted through all my vague hopes and desires and finally selected one that stood out among all others, the impossible dream.

"I have it," I said.

"Yes? Yes?" Dr. Osgood implored.

"I'd like to shoot a world's-record trophy moose!"

Dr. Osgood appeared at that moment to have suffered an infarction of some sort. He rose slowly from his chair, his face twisted in anguish, leaned forward across the desk, and croaked, "Moose? Moose? What do you mean, MOOSE!"

I must admit that my first meeting with Dr. Osgood made me a bit uneasy, but in our later sessions over the years I was able to relax and banter with him about my grades and various other trifles. Often I would leave his office in a state of high good humor, slinging one last witty retort over my shoulder, while Dr. Osgood would put on a show of weeping uncontrollably, at which he was very good. The man could have made his fortune as an actor.

Life in the dorm was not nearly so bad as Mom and Gram had predicted. Oh, sure, occasionally some of the guys would commit a minor atrocity, but nothing out of the ordinary as atrocities go. There were the usual panty raids, water fights, short-sheeting of beds, and dropping of stink bombs into the ventilation system, that sort of innocent fun.

During the first semester of my freshman year I had extremely bad luck with roommates. My first roommate, Wilson Fawfush, flipped out after a few weeks and finally insisted upon being moved to another dorm. The dorm director told me confidentially that Wilson had been suffering from hallucinations, even to the extent of claiming he saw snakes crawling all over the floor of our room.

"Poor Wilson," I said.

"Yes, it's too bad," the director said. "Sometimes the human mind can play strange tricks on us."

"No question about it," I said.

The next roommate assigned me was a real dilly. His name was Lester T. Lillybridge III. It immediately became apparent that Lester had been spoiled rotten as a kid, one result of which was that he had just been expelled from a classy private college back East. His lips seemed to be curled in a permanent sneer of superiority. Scarcely had he dropped his leather-trimmed luggage on the linoleum of our room than we had our first exchange of hostility.

"What are all the guns doing in here?" he asked.

"I'm a hunter," I said.

"Figures," he said. "My parents have arranged this as a punishment for me. What's that ugly thing on the wall?"

His words momentarily crippled my ego. No sooner had I learned I possessed an ego than some fool had to come along and cripple it. "That," I said indignantly, "is a deer head. I mounted it myself."

"Why does it have that stupid grin on its face?"

"That question just goes to show you know nothing about deer," I snapped. "In their natural state, all deer wear stupid grins like that."

Lillybridge laughed evilly. He walked over and kicked a crate I had built in the corner of the room. "What's in there?"

"Snakes," I said.

"Don't be a wise-elbow," Lillybridge said, opening the lid on top and peering in. He slammed down the lid and jumped back. "There *are* snakes in there!"

"Yes."

"Can they get out?"

"Well, they did one night a few weeks ago. That's why I built the crate for them. They can't get out now."

"Geez!" Lillybridge said. "My parents have really done it to me this time!"

Lillybridge found some of the other guys in the dorm more to his liking and spent most of his free time with them, planning and executing various atrocities. When not in class, I spent most of my time in the museum of natural history, where I had a part-time job assisting the curator in various chores. I was thinking of becoming a naturalist. The work was so much fun I would sometimes take it home with me.

"Where's that last batch of snakes we caught?" the curator would ask me.

"I took them home to study," I'd say.

"Well, bring them back!"

Occasionally, the curator would let me try my hand at taxidermy, but the results were never up to his standards. "You didn't do too badly on that ground squirrel," he'd say, "but why does it have that stupid grin on its face?"

During the day, when there were people milling about, the museum was quite pleasant. But at night, when I was there late sweeping the floors or cleaning up a mess of some kind, not always of my own making, the place was downright creepy. The live rattlesnakes in their glass cages, for example, would strike at me, popping the glass with their noses as I walked by. I knew that the snakes couldn't strike through the glass, but my adrenal glands, being ignorant of that fact, would pump a quart or so of adrenaline into my system every time a rattler struck at me. Pretty soon my nerves would be jangling, and shadows would seem to dart and dance among the displays. The huge, mounted timber wolf would blink his eyes as I scurried by with my dust cloth. The mounted cougar would lash its tail. The bobcat would twitch its whiskers.

There was one particularly loathsome room that I had to venture into in order to empty the various waste receptacles, some of which occasionally held startling surprises. This was the dissection room, where dead animals were prepared for whatever purpose the curator had in mind for them. One large glass case contained a kind of carnivorous beetle, thousands of them, used for cleaning the flesh off bones, leaving them shiny clean. I would imagine I could hear the beetles at their work, performing a grim symphony with their infinitesimal *chomp-chomp-chomps*. Between the rattlesnakes and the beetles, my late night chores in the museum would often leave me in a state of barely controlled terror.

The dissection room contained a dingy gray freezer about the size and shape of a coffin, only somewhat deeper. I often wondered what it might hold. One night when I was there alone, my curiosity overpowered my terror sufficiently for me to peek in. Ever so carefully I raised the lid, feeling the beat of my heart in every single goose bump on my body. Bit by bit, with cold sweat flooding off of me, I raised one eyelid. Nothing! The freezer was empty.

At that moment I thought of an atrocity to commit.

I had happened to mention to Lester, as we lay in our bunks one night, that my nerves were a bit frazzled from my work at the museum. He had laughed in his nasty, evil way and expressed the opinion that I was "just chicken." Confiding my fear to a person like Lilly-bridge had been nothing less than a lapse of sanity on my part. He had soon told all the other guys on our floor, most of whom up to that moment had regarded me with a certain amount of trepidation. Now they began to feel that I was a safe subject upon which to perform their practical jokes. This was a theory in need of puncturing.

I set my trap for Lillybridge with great care. First I wrote on a sheet of paper the message, "Dr. Smith, please finish with the dissection of this cadaver as soon as possible. It's beginning to spoil."

Then I waited until late one night when Lillybridge and I were in our bunks exchanging a few nasty barbs with each other before going to sleep.

"Let's be serious for a moment, Lester," I said.

"I am being serious, worm wit," he replied.

"Naw, come on, I mean it. I've got to tell somebody about this. It's really getting to me. I may even have to quit my job in the museum because of it."

"So, what is it, mussel mouth? You can tell your old Uncle Lester anything in complete confidence. Har! Har! Har!"

"Well, you see, there's this freezer in the dissection room at the museum. It's about the size and shape of a coffin. And I'm dying to look into it. I just have this uncontrollable compulsion to see what's inside. But I'm scared of what I'll find. I'm torn between my fear and my curiosity. I just can't stand it any more!"

"Har har har har har har har har!" Lester said. "Har har har."

"And what I was wondering, Lester, is if maybe you and I could sneak out to the museum right now and open that freezer. I've got a key."

"Sure!" he said. "Sounds like fun!"

"No kidding, Lester? You promise you won't chicken out? That no matter what, you'll open the freezer? I'd hate to have to tell the guys that you were afraid to open the freezer!"

"Let's go," Lester said, bounding out of his bunk.

After checking to make sure the campus security police were nowhere in sight, I unlocked the door to the

museum and we slipped inside. I told Lester we couldn't
turn on any lights because that would alert campus
security to our presence. We'd just have to make do with
the lights from the display cases, which cast an eerie glow
about the room.

"You're not getting nervous are you, Lester?" I
asked, as we worked our way through the museum.

"Har! Har! Har!" Lester laughed.

I led him up alongside the rattlesnake case. Lester
stared dully at the snakes. Then, *buzzzzz-buzzzzz pop! pop!
pop!* The snakes hit the glass a few inches from his face.

As soon as he had stopped dancing up and down,
Lester said, "You should have told me they were alive!
How was I to know they would strike at me!" I could see
the level of adrenaline rising through his eyes.

We moved on a ways. "What's that behind you?" I
asked suddenly. Lester spun around to stare the timber
wolf in the fangs. Even in the soft glow of the display
lights, I thought I could see outward signs of Lester's
heart ricocheting around his rib cage. "Oh, just an ol'
timber wolf," I said. "Nothing to be afraid of." By now, I
calculated that Lester's circulation system was pumping
about 80 percent adrenaline. And I hadn't even shown
him the carnivorous beetles yet.

When we reached the door of the windowless
dissection room, I told Lester to wait outside until I had
gone in and turned on the light. He didn't argue. I
slipped in and placed my note on top of the freezer, then
flipped the wall switch. The lights came on in a blinding
glare. Then I opened the door and motioned Lester in.

"Here's something you might find interesting, Lester," I said, in the manner of a tour guide. "These beetles
are used to clean all the flesh off skeletons. Gee, I wonder
what they are working on now."

Lester stared at the quivering black mass of beetles, his eyes widening in horror.

"Hear their tiny little *chomp-chomps?*" I asked.

"Yeh," Lester said weakly.

I turned and pulled Lester stumbling along behind me. "Now over here we have the freezer. Looks sorta like a coffin, doesn't it? Maybe now you can see why it gives me the creeps. Can't tell what might be in there, but I've got this terrible compulsion to find out! How about you, Lester?"

"Hunh?"

"Boy am I glad you came along to open up the freezer for me, Lester. But what have we here? Seems to be a note. Dang! I forgot my spectacles! Read it for me, will you, Lester?"

Lester's eyes fastened on the note like a matched set of vises. "*Good jumpin' gosh almighty*," he hissed through his teeth, something that's not that easy to do even in the best of times.

"Well, forget the note, we're wasting time," I said. "Go ahead and pop her open, and let's see what's inside."

"N-no!" Lester said.

"C'mon!" I said. "Quit kidding around! Flip up the ol' lid there!"

"Un-unh," Lester said, shaking his head.

"You mean you're too chicken to open the freezer?" I asked.

"Un-hunh," Lester said, nodding affirmatively.

"Har! Har! Har!" I replied. "Too chicken to open a measly old freezer! Wait till the guys hear about this! I guess I'll just have to open it myself!"

I grabbed the lid and flipped it up, watching Lester's face all the while in order to record every detail of his reaction so I'd be able to provide the guys in the dorm with an accurate report. There was, for instance, this little popping motion of his eyeballs as he stared into the open freezer. Then there was the way his jaw sagged and a bit of drool rolled over his lower lip. Overall, there was the general response of someone accidentally sticking a finger in an empty light socket. The effect was even better than I had hoped for.

"Har! Har! Har!" I laughed. "There, you see, it's empty!" I turned to point into the freezer. "Har! Har! HAAAAAAARRRRRRR!"

Ol' Lester may have been a spoiled brat, but he sure knew how to run. I counted at least three times that he passed me on our way back to the dorm.

Later, I learned that, unbeknownst to me, the curator had stored a dead black bear in the freezer, its skin partially peeled off.

Lester and I went on to become good friends, and that winter I even taught him how to trap muskrat, just in case he ever ran short of money. He changed into as nice a guy as you would ever want to meet. It seemed as if the scare at the museum had purged all the meanness and smugness and arrogance out of Lester. Heck, I was even a little purged myself.

The Gift

☞ ☞ ☞Christmas is an uneasy time for me. Maybe it's because my father was a practical joker. When I was small he would tell me that if I didn't behave myself Santa would fill my stocking with kindling sticks and rotten potatoes. I would try to behave myself but could never seem to get the hang of it. Christmas thus became a matter of great apprehension to me, because even though I couldn't behave I wasn't stupid, and I figured Santa Claus had to have my name on some kindling and rotten potatoes. Sure enough, come Christmas morning I would creep out of bed, peek around the corner at my stocking, and there would be some kindling sticks protruding from it, along with a few sprouts from rotten potatoes.

"AAIIIGHHHHHHH!" I would exclaim.

"Ho, ho, ho!" my father would laugh.

Then, of course, he would show me that under the kindling sticks and rotten potatoes were a ball, a top, some dominoes, a tin soldier, and maybe some candy orange slices. I would punish him by playing all day with kindling and potatoes. We didn't have psychology in those days; otherwise, I might have been emotionally scarred for life by my father's little trick. As it is, I become uneasy at Christmastime.

One of the reasons I become uneasy is the cost of things I put in my own kids' stockings: digital watches, rock-concert tickets, skiing lessons, and the like. Fortunately, the kindling sticks and rotten potatoes don't cost much and never fail to give me a good laugh. There's nothing funnier than teenagers dumping out their stockings and exclaiming, "AAIIIGHHHHHHHH!" They exclaim that when they discover the stocking doesn't contain a set of keys to a new car.

Probably the main reason for my unease, however, is the gifts I receive for Christmas. Whenever the kids ask my wife what to get Ol' Whosis for Christmas, she tells them, "You know how he loves outdoor sports. Why don't you get him something outdoorsie?"

"Good idea," they cry in unison. "How much can he afford for us to get him?"

Let me state here that there should be a law prohibiting any person who uses the term "outdoorsie" from dispensing advice about what kinds of presents to buy an outdoorsman. A few years ago, after my spouse advised her I would like something outdoorsie, one of my wealthy aunts gave me something called the Ultimate Fishing Machine. As near as I could make out from the operational manual, you stayed at home and watched TV while the UFM went out and caught the fish, cleaned them, cooked them, and ate them. When it got back home, you asked the UFM what kind of luck it had and it told you lies.

The manufacturer claimed in his literature that the Ultimate Fishing Machine had been made possible through the miracle of miniaturization. I would have preferred a miracle that assembled the machine before passing it on to me. At the very least, the company could have miniaturized an engineer and enclosed him in the package to help put the UFM together.

I never even attempted to assemble the Ultimate Fishing Machine and so cannot report on its competence at fishing. Bothersome as it may be, I'd just as soon go to the trouble of catching, cleaning, cooking, and eating my own fish. If I work at it, I can probably even learn to tell fishing lies.

Nothing gladdens the heart of a sporting-goods store proprietor more than to be approached by a lady who says something like, "My husband is the outdoorsie type. I wonder if you might suggest a suitable Christmas gift for him."

The proprietor grins evilly and rumples his hair so as to conceal the horns protruding just above his temples. Here is his chance to revenge himself on one of the arrogant sportsmen who have snorted derisively and even guffawed openly at certain items of the proprietor's stock.

"Here's something fishermen are absolutely crazy about," he says. "The musical fishing creel! Every time a fish is inserted, it plays Beethoven's Fifth Symphony. If they go over their limit, Elvis Presley sings 'I Ain't Nothin' but a Hound Dog.' "

"Marvelous!" the wife exclaims. "I'll take it! Any other suggestions?"

"Now here's a nifty item—a pair of sleeping-bag warmers for backpackers."

"They look like bricks."

"That's what they are—but not just your ordinary bricks. No ma'am. These are special high-density bricks —just feel how heavy they are. The way they work, the backpacker heats them in the campfire and then inserts them in his sleeping bag. Keep him toasty warm all night."

"What a nice idea," the wife says. "I'll take a set."

"How about a gag gift for the fellow who likes to go out exploring by himself in the wilds—a trick compass. See, every time you look at it, North shifts to a different direction. Ha! Ha! It comes with maps that instantly dissolve when they come in contact with cold sweat. The compass and maps together are sold as The $8.95 Do-It-Yourself Divorce Kit."

"It's tempting," the wife says, "but I'd better not."

"Here's a nice gift for the man who has nothing," the proprietor tells her. "A tiny inflatable vest for grasshoppers. Keeps them afloat, and with this little harness to fasten them to the hook, they can be used over and over until a fish takes them or they die of old age."

"That is absolutely *darling!*" the wife exclaims. "I'll take two."

"Did I show you the grasshopper water skis . . . ?"

There are other reasons for my unease at Christmas.

After my father died, Christmas was a rather bleak occasion at our house for a number of years. I got a foreshadowing of just how bleak one Christmas was going to be when my mother warned me, "If you don't behave, all Santa is going to put in your stocking is kindling sticks."

"What about the rotten potatoes?" I asked.

"He can't afford them this year," she said.

Santa always seemed to come through with something though, even if it was pre-owned, as they say. I would get some used clothes, used books, used toys, used candy. It was my sister, the Troll, who gave me the used candy.

"This Snickers bar has teeth marks on it," I said.

"I know," the Troll said. "I forgot, I don't like caramel."

"You didn't lick it all over, did you?" I asked, examining the bar carefully for lick marks.

"No," she said. "What kind of a person do you think I am?"

Thinking that she was the kind of a person who would lick a Christmas present, I worried for weeks after eating the candy bar that I would come down with some terrible disease carried by sisters.

Even back when I was nine or ten I was known as an outdoorsie type among the relatives. Rich Aunt Maude wrote my mother and asked what kind of outdoorsie present I would like for Christmas. My mother wrote back that I would "just love something related to fishing." We speculated for weeks whether Maude would send me a fine fishing rod or a fine reel or a tackle box filled with tackle. I thought possibly she might even come through with a boat, motor, and trailer. When the gift arrived though, the boat, motor, and trailer were instantly ruled out because of the package's minuscule dimensions, so minuscule in fact that they also ruled out the fine fishing rod, reel, and tackle box. I figured all it could be was a fly book filled up with expensive flies. Christmas morning we all got up and rushed down to the Christmas bush, and the family waited with bated breath—mouthwash being unknown to us in those days—as I tore open the package from rich Aunt Maude. Even to this day I can recall my response upon unveiling the present:

"AAIIIGHHHHHHHH!"

There, lying in state before me in a monogrammed box with glittering foil wrapping and soft crinkly tissue paper were . . . *two silk neckties* . . . *with pictures of fish on them!*

"Don't be so upset," my mother pleaded, pulling me down off the wall. "You can wear them with your new suit—whenever you get a new suit."

"And whenever you get a neck," the Troll added. "Now open my present!"

"What is it?" I said, my bitterness ebbing.

The Troll smiled sweetly. "Gum."

I must say it was pretty good gum, too. There was still a lot of flavor left in it.

My mother always used to say that we should be grateful for whatever we received. "Just think," she would admonish us, "there are millions of people all over the country living in poverty, who can't even afford popcorn to decorate their Christmas bush with."

I tried not to think of the poor people as I decorated the bush. "How does this look?" I would ask as I stepped back to study my placement of the popcorn.

"Why not put it right up on the tip?" the Troll would suggest. "That way it'll look like a little tiny white star."

The only poor person I knew at that time was Rancid Crabtree, the old woodsman who lived at the foot of the mountain about a mile from our place. I spent a large part of my early life following Rancid around and studying him and learning all sorts of interesting things. But Rancid was poor. He didn't seem to know that he was poor, however, and I never had the heart to tell him, because he was the happiest person I'd ever met. If he had known he was poor, of course, then he would have been sad and miserable all the time. As it was, Rancid was able to live out his whole life in blissful ignorance of the fact that he was poor.

A few days before Christmas one year, I wandered over to Rancid's cabin to see what he was up to. He was carrying an armload of firewood into the cabin and invited me in. I looked around, expecting to see a Christmas bush with some presents under it. There was nothing but the rumpled bed, the old barrel stove, a table and some broken chairs, rusty traps, a shotgun and some rifles on wall pegs, and a few other odds and ends.

"Where's your Christmas bush?" I asked him.

"If Ah was to have anythang, it 'ud be a Crimmas *tree*. But Ah don't see why Ah got to brang a tree into the house when all Ah's got to do is look out the winder and see all of 'ems Ah want."

"But what do you put all your presents under?" I persisted.

Rancid stared at me for a long moment, then snorted. "Ah use to git all kinds of presents. They'd be piled up n'ar to the ceilin' and Ah be kickin' an' stumblin' over 'em all the time. So finally Ah just up an' tells folks to shet off givin' me all them presents. Ya know, Ah ain't missed 'em one bit. A man jist outgrows presents, Ah guess."

I hoped I'd never outgrow presents, and while I was thinking about that, a great wave of sorrow crashed down upon me and poured right down into the insides of my feet and filled up my toes and then came welling back up again into my throat.

"What's wrong with you, boy?" Rancid said.

"Your stove is smoking," I choked. "I better get some fresh air," and I bolted out the door.

Rancid came out on the porch and watched me as I gasped cold air into my lungs.

That was when the great idea occurred to me.

"Say, Rancid," I said, "why don't you come have Christmas dinner with us at our house?"

"Naw, Ah couldn't do thet. You know yer ol' granny an' me don't git along."

"Why, it was her who told me to invite you," I lied. "She said to me, 'Now you go give Rancid Crabtree an invite to Christmas dinner!'"

"Wall, dad-gum maw hide! Shore! You tell her Ah'd be happy as a hawg at a hangin' to shar' yer Crimmas vittles with y'alls."

When I told Mom that I had invited Rancid to Christmas dinner, she said she didn't know if we could afford the extra expense.

"Heck, he won't eat that much," I said.

"The expense I'm talking about is repairing the hole in the roof when your grandmother goes through it."

Gram didn't go through the roof when she heard the news about Rancid. She took it rather well as a matter of fact, as soon as she got done hopping up and down in the middle of the kitchen and saying "AAIIIGHHHH!"

"Good gosh almighty, boy, do you know what you've done? That Rancid Crabtree ain't took a bath since he fell in the crick in '27. Folks pay him just to walk by their farms so the smell will drive the ticks off their critters. And you invite him to Christmas dinner! Well, all we can do is put the extra leaves in the table and set you and him down at the far end!"

"Hoooray!" I shouted. "I'll even help get things ready. How many extra leaves we got for the table, Gram?"

Gram shook her head. "Not nearly enough, boy, not nearly enough!"

Personally, I didn't think that Rancid smelled all that bad, but there was a story told that his approach from an upwind direction had once raised an alarm that the stockyards had caught on fire. In any case, there was a great deal of moaning and groaning among the women-folk that Rancid's presence at Christmas dinner would be a lingering one. The Troll practiced eating with her nose pinched together, and Gram and Mom debated whether we should eat with all the windows open and hope a blizzard would come up and provide a strong cross draft.

All of this carrying on began to worry me, because I didn't want to ruin Christmas dinner for the rest of the family. So, the day before Christmas I hastened through the snow to Rancid's cabin with the notion of persuading him that coming to dinner might not be such a good idea after all. Upon approaching the cabin, however, I noticed great white clouds rising from the doors and windows and cracks in the roof. I thought the place was on fire, and ran yelling for Rancid to get out of the cabin.

Rancid stuck his head out of a steam cloud. "What in tarnation is all the ruckus about?"

I peeked past him into the cabin. There was a great tub on top of the barrel stove, which was belching out smoke and flames on all sides, and the clouds of steam were boiling up from the tub.

"Whatcha got in the tub?" I asked.

Rancid shuddered. "Water. Ah'm gonna do somethin' Ah ain't did since '27. It's a torture to me, but Ah'm gonna do it jist fer you. Ah hope you appreciate it. An' don't never ast me to do it ag'in, 'cause Ah ain't!"

"Oh, I won't, I won't never ask you to do it again, Rancid." I turned to sprint happily back to my house. "See you at Christmas dinner tomorrow!"

When I burst into the kitchen, Gram was just removing from the oven a batch of cinnamon rolls.

"You don't have to worry about eating with the windows open at Christmas dinner tomorrow," I told her.

"Oh? Rancid ain't comin'?"

"He's coming all right, but this very moment he's fixing us up a nice surprise."

"A gift! Land sakes alive, we didn't think to get that dirty ol' rascal anything!"

"Well, it's not exactly . . ."

Gram slapped a hot cinnamon roll out of my hand. "Don't tell me exactly. I'll just wrap up these cinnamon rolls for him. Ain't nobody gives us a present we don't give him a present back!"

"But . . ."

"No but's!"

Christmas day, as we waited for Rancid to show up for dinner, Mom said, "I'd feel better about this if we already had all the windows open when he came. That way we wouldn't be so likely to hurt his feelings."

"That's the way I feel about it, too," Gram said. "And we should of put the extra leaves in the table."

Suddenly, the Troll, who had been looking out the window, shouted, "Here he comes! And wow! You're not going to believe this!"

There was a knock on the door, and Mom called out, "Come right on in, Rancid!"

In burst Rancid with a big snaggletoothed grin. "Surprise!" he shouted.

And were we surprised? Why, you could have knocked every last one of us over with a feather!

As soon as Mom had recovered from her astonishment enough to speak, she said, "Rancid, why don't you throw open a few of those windows over there and let in some fresh air while we put the extra leaves in the table. Then I want to get a better look at those skis."

"Steamed the curve into the tips mawsef," Rancid said proudly. "Put a couple birch boards in a tub of water on top of maw stove and them ol' tips bent up jist as purty as you please. Ain't made a pa'r of skis since '27."

"A mite wider on that window, if you please,

Rancid," Gram said. "My, don't that blizzard feel good! Now let me feast my eyes on them skis."

"Thar fer the boy," Rancid said. "But Ah made them big nuff y'all can use 'em if ya wants."

That was one of the finest Christmas gifts and one of the finest Christmas dinners I have ever known. As Mom said as we sat shivering happily around the table, "It's a chill wind that blows no warmth."

The Sensuous Angler

☞ ☞ ☞ There would be a lot less divorce in this country if more husbands and wives fished together. Spouses that fish together stay together.

My wife, Bun, for example, used to absolutely detest fishing. Whenever I dragged her out on the lake, she would sit there in the boat with her eyes fixed on me in an unblinking stare that I often imagined to be almost murderous. From time to time I'd even speak a few kind words to her in an effort to break the spell: "Row a bit faster along here, will you, Bun? I don't want my lure to get snagged in the weeds." Of course, there are some people who just don't respond to kind words, and Bun seemed to be one of them.

Besides my compulsive interest in fishing, what complicated our marital situation even more was that women find me extraordinarily attractive. "Irresistible" would not be too strong a word. I sometimes have to laugh to myself at the great show they put on to make me think they're totally unaware of my existence. Just recently I was sitting next to a beautiful woman on the uptown bus. I could tell she was flustered by the way she rummaged around in her purse, finally dug out a compact, and started fixing her face. It was absolutely hilarious, particularly when she wiped off some excess eye shadow with the tip of my tie. I mean, there are no lengths to which women will not go in their pretense of ignoring me!

Bun, quite forgivably, used to be terribly jealous. I'd try to kid her out of it. When we would come home from grocery shopping, I'd say, "Did you see how that cute blonde at the store was pretending to ignore me? I nearly laughed out loud!"

"There's only one can of tuna here," Bun would say. "I could have sworn I bought two cans of tuna."

That's how bad it was. Mad, uncontrollable jealousy was practically destroying our marriage.

The combination of my obsession with fishing and my irresistible appeal to women took a more extreme turn for the worse one day when Bun discovered a reddish smudge on the collar of one of my white dress shirts.

"Aha, I've got you now, you rascal," she snarled. "What's this red smudge on your shirt collar?"

How had I ever managed to overlook that smudge? My mind raced, feverishly searching for a plausible lie.

"It's probably just a lipstick smudge from one of the girls at the office," I tried.

"Ha!" Bun snapped. "I wasn't born yesterday, you know! This is salmon-egg juice! Here I think you're down at the office working, and actually you're sneaking off to go fishing. You've probably rented a secret apartment where you keep an extra set of fishing gear!"

"But there's this other woman . . ." That's as far as I

got. If there's one thing I can't stand about Bun, it's the way she expresses her jealousy by laughing uncontrollably.

Actually, there *was* another woman. Her name was Jennifer, and she worked in the same advertising agency I did. There was something about her that made it almost impossible for me to keep my eyes off of her. As with most women, she made a great show of ignoring my existence. There was that time, for instance, when I was standing by the coat rack and she tried to hang her coat on me. Of course she had laughed in an embarrassed way, but not until she had made repeated efforts to keep her coat from slipping off my shoulders.

My job at the agency was to invent benevolent lies about a client's product. So distracted was I by Jennifer that one day I allowed a truth to slip into my copy and was nearly fired. Naturally, I was upset by the mishap, and as soon as the boss had gone down to the shop to resharpen his reamer, I whipped out my portable fly-tying outfit and began to tie a few Royal Henchmen to soothe my nerves. Suddenly I felt a pair of eyes on me. At first I thought it was Charley Fife, playing another one of his grotesque practical jokes. Then I realized it was Jennifer watching me. She came over to my desk.

"Hello," she said, holding out a hand. "I'm Jennifer. You must be new here."

"Oh, I've been here awhile," I replied suavely.

"How long?"

"Four years."

"Strange that I've never noticed you before. Our desks are only twenty feet apart."

"Yes, well *I've* noticed you, Jennifer."

"You have? Anything in particular."

"Is there ever!" I breathed. "For one thing, there's the way you read *Field & Stream* so avidly at lunch while the other girls are gawking at *Glamour*. Then I saw the way you took that casting reel apart and put it back together when you were supposed to be typing the annual report."

"Oh dear!" she cried, tittering. "You caught me in the act, did you? I was just cleaning my Protron Ninety Double-Widget Power-Glide Pro-Caster."

"You're telling me!" I said. "You have about the prettiest little Pro-Caster I've ever laid eyes on."

A flush of embarrassment filled Jennifer's cheeks, reminding me of the red-bellies I used to catch in the creek behind our house when I was a kid. As she bent over to whisper in my ear, I detected the faint, lingering fragrance of OFF! "Did you notice anything else?" Her voice was husky.

"You mean . . . the way you rewrapped the split bamboo rod during your coffee breaks last February? Of course I noticed! It nearly drove me wild!"

She smiled. "You're really a very attract . . . You're not that bad look . . . I like large ears a lot, I really do."

I chuckled. The poor girl was practically tongue-tied.

"What attracted me to you most, though," she continued, "was your little portable fly-tying outfit. It's lovely! Say, I've got an idea. Why don't you stop by my place tonight and we'll . . . well, you know?"

"I know!" I said. "I know!"

After I had slipped into Jennifer's apartment that evening, she poured us each a glass of wine and turned on the stereo. Then we got right down to business. I was amazed, I must tell you, at what that woman knew. In fifteen minutes she taught me more about how to cure fresh steelhead eggs for bait than all the grizzled old anglers I've ever known. Such was our mad frenzy of curing steelhead eggs that some of the juice apparently splashed on my collar. That was the spot my wife detected.

"No one must ever find out about us," I told Jennifer as we shook hands at the door of her apartment as I was leaving.

"Oh, I know, I know," she said. "But next time, next time . . ."

"What?" I gasped. "Tell me what, Jennifer!"

"Next time . . . I'll show you how to filet perch!"

I was puzzled. "But, Jennifer, I know how to filet perch."

She gave me a lascivious smile. "Not the way *I* do it."

My imagination did a wild dance, raising goose bumps on my flesh the size of bongo drums. "When can we do it?" I asked. "When can we filet perch together?"

"Maybe next Tuesday night. Call me after eight. But if a man's voice answers, hang up."

"A man's voice?"

"Yes, my husband's. He is very big, with a short temper. And he hates fishing and fish. It would be most unfortunate for you if he caught us—you know—fileting together."

I shuddered at the image conjured up by her warning.

It was a long week. Every time I looked up, I saw Jennifer typing reports a few yards away. I could scarcely tear my eyes away from her flying fingers, those very fingers which, but a few days before, I had watched . . . had watched knead alum into a sinewy mess of steelhead eggs. Once a man, an angler, has experienced that with a woman, there is no turning back. And she had this lovely way of tossing her head. It reminded me of the way a fly fisher, hands filled with rod and line, will toss his head in order to shake a deer fly off his nose. It was beautiful.

At home during supper, I found myself staring absently at my plate. All I could think about was fileting with Jennifer.

"What's wrong with Pop?" one of the kids asked one evening. "How come he doesn't tell us those stupid stories about his childhood any more?"

"Don't complain," their mother said. "Your father has important things on his mind."

"We ain't complaining!" the kids said in unison. "We ain't complaining!"

"Have some respect!" I shouted at them. "I never once talked to one of my parents like that! Why, one time when I was only eight years old and had just walked the fifteen miles home from school in knee-deep snow . . ."

"Forget I mentioned it," the first kid said.

After supper Bun followed me into my den, also jestingly referred to as "the hole under the stairs." She put her hands on my shoulders and said, "Something's wrong. I know something's wrong. You get upset over the smallest things. I saw the way your eyes became all teary when you couldn't stab that last pea with your fork at supper. You can tell me! What's wrong?"

"Nothing's wrong," I said. What made me feel so bad about my affair with Jennifer is that Bun's a great wife. Sure, she has her faults. There was that time she screamed as if she had found Jack the Ripper in our refrigerator instead of merely a mayonnaise jar containing live hellgrammites. Heck, Jennifer would never have screamed at the sight of a few crummy live hellgrammites.

The truth was that Jennifer didn't really stand a chance of coming between my wife and me. Ol' Bun and I had just been through too many things together. She had stuck with me through thin and thin. The only thing to do, I told myself, was to try to forget Jennifer. But I couldn't.

When Tuesday night rolled around, I slipped out to a pay phone and called Jennifer's number. Jennifer answered.

"Is it all right?" I asked.

"Yes," she said, breathlessly. "Hammer is flying out of town on a business trip tonight and won't be back until tomorrow."

"Great!" I said. "I'll sneak right over."

I told Bun I was going to spend the evening with the boys down at Kelly's Bar & Grill and not to expect me home too early. She said fine, that she would leave the key under the cushion on the porch swing. I was halfway over to Jennifer's before it occurred to me that there isn't a cushion on the porch swing. We don't even have a porch swing. We scarcely have a porch. I wondered if Bun suspected anything.

A sudden thought jolted me: *Hammer? Her husband's name is Hammer?*

When Jennifer met me at the door, I was disappointed to find her dressed in a low-cut, filmy negligee.

"You're early," she said. "Mix yourself a drink while I slip into something a little more comfortable." Presently she returned from the bedroom dressed in baggy, patched fishing pants and a plaid wool shirt sprinkled with fish scales.

"Hey hey hey!" I said. "Now that's more like it!" I thrust a package into her hands. "By the way, here's a little something for you."

Her hands tore eagerly at the wrappings. Nervously, I wondered if maybe I had made a mistake, giving her such a personal gift so soon in our relationship.

"Oh!" she cried, clapping her hands together in

delight. "They're beautiful! You shouldn't have! They must have cost you a small fortune!"

"Nope," I said, smiling modestly. "I caught them myself. Off the old Grand Street fishing pier. Do you really like them?"

Jennifer wiped her joy-streaked cheeks on her shirt sleeve. "Oh, I love them! They are absolutely gorgeous perch! All Hammer ever gives me are long-stemmed red roses and dumb furs."

It was obvious her husband was either a thoughtless clod or totally insensitive. Some men just don't know how to treat a woman!

Overcome by the excitement of the moment, Jennifer and I rushed into the kitchen and began to filet madly. Never have I known a woman who could filet like Jennifer! Perch after perch fell under her flashing knife. I became mesmerized by her very motions, the way she whacked off the heads, stripped away the skins, and sliced off the filets. Time ceased to exist for me, and all space seemed confined to Jennifer's laminated maple chopping block.

Then the earth moved.

"Did the earth move for you, Jennifer?" I asked.

"Yes yes yes yes yes!" she cried. "And do you know what made it move?"

"What?"

"Hammer! He always trips on that last step at the top of the stairs!"

"HAMMER?" I yelled. "I thought you said he was away on business!"

"Maybe he missed his flight! Maybe he suspects something! But that is Hammer coming down the hall!"

Now I could feel the earth move with every step Hammer took down the hallway. The steps sounded angry.

"What'll we do?" I hissed at Jennifer.

"What do you mean 'we,' you burglar you!" she snapped.

Somehow I felt that Jennifer had chosen that moment to break off our relationship. Very soon I expected her husband to break off more than that.

"Look at the evidence!" I hissed, as Hammer rattled his key in the lock. "He'll know we've been fileting together. No matter what you tell him, he'll know a burglar didn't break into the apartment and force you to filet!"

Jennifer scooped up all the evidence and flung it into the freezing compartment of the refrigerator.

"Jen?" called out Hammer, his voice rumbling into the kitchen like a slow freight.

A second before Hammer's shadow fell upon us, Jennifer lunged across the kitchen, threw her arms around me, and planted a big, wet, utterly disgusting kiss on my mustache. And then Hammer filled the doorway.

"Who dis?" he demanded, pointing at me with a finger the size of a zucchini.

"Oh," said Jennifer, "this is just one of my professors from night school who heard you were going to be out of town tonight and thought he'd sneak by."

"You 'spect me to buy a cock'n'bull story like dat? It smells fishy in here! You two been up to somethin' wid fish, ain'tcha? Filetin'! I'll bet the two of you have been filetin' behind my back. Or maybe even, even—I can't stand the thought of it—curin' steelhead eggs for bait! As soon as I leave town to do a little job for the Godfather . . ."

"No, no, Hammy, it wasn't anything like that," Jennifer cried. "Please don't kill him!"

"Repeat that last part, would you, Jennifer?" I whispered to her. "I don't think Hammy heard it."

At that moment Hammer blinked, giving me the opportunity to leap out the kitchen window and sprint to safety down the alley. When I finally stopped to catch my breath, I made up my mind right then and there that never again was I going to filet with another man's wife, particularly one whose apartment was higher than the ground floor. For one thing, it's so darn hard to sprint to safety with your legs protruding from your armpits.

I had learned my lesson about other women and decided that the thing to do was to give my own wife more instruction in the art of fileting. That way she might even learn to enjoy the sport. And the very next weekend I started her lessons.

"All right, Bun," I instructed, "just remember that balance is everything. There, you've nearly got it. Raise your right arm a bit more. Good. Now you've got the idea! Heck, you could carry the canoe all day like that if you had to. Get started toward the lake now, and I'll grab my fly rod and be right along behind."

Bun still isn't too enthusiastic about fishing yet. As a matter of fact, just the other day when we were out on the river she said if I would forget about the idea of making her my fishing pal, she wouldn't complain about another woman or two.

Not a chance! "Listen, Bun," I said, "you're the only woman for me, and I'm going to make you love fishing if it's the last thing you do."

I could have sworn that she was so touched by this remark that a single tear trickled down her cheek. It was hard to tell for sure, though, because of the cloud of mosquitoes around her.

And Now
Stay Tuned for
"The Camp Chef"

☞ ☞ ☞**A** friend of mine, Fred Flim, is a television producer, and at lunch a while back I suggested to him that what the tube needs now is a show about camp cookery. Scarcely able to conceal his enthusiasm for such a show, Fred pretended to be totally absorbed in an effort to suck the pimento out of a martini olive.

"Great concept, hunh?" I said.

"Fantastic," Fred said. "Hey, man, can you believe those Yankees! What a team! After those first two games, I would have . . ."

"You really like the idea that much?" I said, almost overcome by excitement. "You're not just putting me on? Wow! I hope you're not just saying this because we're such good friends."

Fred turned serious, his gravity only slightly lessened by his having clenched a large, pitless green olive grotesquely in his eye. "May I have this dance, Miss?" he asked me, hunching his neck down into his shoulders and reaching out with two bread sticks protruding from his sleeves. People who are not friends of Fred's often have difficulty telling when he's being serious.

I chuckled appreciatively at his little performance and told him that it reminded me of the time his wife thought he was on a three-day fishing trip with me but wasn't and what a kick she'd get out of the story.

Fred plucked the olive from his eye and put the bread sticks back in their basket. "What are you thinking of calling this show of yours?" he asked.

" 'The Camp Chef,' " I replied. "It will be kind of an outdoorsie 'The French Chef' but with me as the star instead of Julia Child."

"Fantastic," he said. "Really fantastic. It sort of gets a person right here."

"How come there?"

"Well, I was never very knowledgeable about anatomy. Tell you what, you work up a script and get the necessary props together and be down at the studio at ten sharp Monday morning and we'll shoot a pilot of 'The Camp Chef.' "

"Fantastic!" I said, just to show Fred I was already picking up on the technical jargon.

"By the way," he said, "you don't happen to know any reliable hit men, do you?"

"No, I don't," I replied. "Anyway, the hit-man concept has been worked to death on television. I'd scrap that idea if I were you."

Fred smiled thinly and drummed his fingers on the table. I could tell he was already calculating the Nielsen ratings on "The Camp Chef."

I was a little late getting to the studio on Monday. For some unknown reason, my brakes failed just as I was approaching the steep, winding stretch of highway between my home and the television studio. The mechanic at the garage said it looked as if my brake line had been sabotaged, but I told him that was ridiculous. Then, while I was hoofing back to the house to get my camper truck, some idiot in a big black sedan nearly ran over me—twice!—which was odd, since I was walking across a cow pasture at the time.

Anyway, I was late getting to the studio, and I guess Fred had just about given up on me, because he seemed more than a little astonished when I showed up carrying all my props.

"Boy," I told him by way of explanation, "you just can't hire competent help anymore."

"You're telling *me!*" Fred interrupted.

"Yeah," I went on, "I had this guy do some repair work on my car last week, and the incompetent fool accidentally filed my brake line nearly in half. Lucky I wasn't killed."

"Hmmmmmm," Fred said. "What's all that junk you got in the gunnysack there, anyway?"

"These are the props for my show, 'The Camp Chef.' "

Fred shook his head. "Gee, I'm really sorry, but I forgot that we were going to do a pilot of your show today. All the studios are being used."

"That's all right, Fred, ol' buddy," I said. "Think nothing of it. Danged if it doesn't remind me of that time you were supposed to be on a three-day fishing trip with me but . . ."

Fred picked up a phone. "Clear Studio Five," he snarled. "We need it for a show on camp cookery. . . . That's right—*camp cookery!* Are you deaf or something!"

Just as we were stepping into the studio, a concrete block dropped from the darkness above us and crashed at my feet. It was a close call, and I must say I've never seen Fred more upset. Glaring up into the shadows, he screamed, "Not *here*, you meathead, not *here!*" I could tell this wasn't one of Fred's better days either.

Knowing that time is money in the television business, I immediately dragged my sack of props out to a lighted platform in front of the cameras and started to get everything arranged. I had studied Julia Child's technique for many years and consequently was quite familiar with the format, as they say, of cooking shows.

I quickly organized my cooking ingredients, utensils, and props, using as a table a piece of television equipment that didn't seem to be in use at the moment. My friend Retch Sweeney showed up about then, dragging several dried-up Christmas trees and a red-faced receptionist.

"You can't haul that junk in here," the receptionist whined.

"Where do ya want these trees, Pat?" Retch asked.

"Arrange them around the set," I said. "It's all right, Miss," I told the receptionist. "He's with me."

"Who are you?" she asked.

"I'm with Fred," I explained.

"Gee, I dunno," she said. "I better call the guard."

"Ha! Ha!" I laughed. "That reminds me of a funny story. One time Fred was supposed to be on a three-day fishing trip with me . . ."

"Oh, no!" she responded. "I remember you now! Yeah, come to think of it, Fred did tell me about your idea for a show."

"I bet he said to take good care of me, too, didn't he?"

"Gosh, I dunno. I thought he said he had arranged for somebody else to take care of you."

"Good ol' Fred," I said. "It would be hard to find a more considerate guy."

Even though dried out, Retch's trees gave a nice woodsy effect to the set.

Two cameramen came into the studio, yawning and scratching themselves, and started pushing the television cameras into position. I could see Fred in the director's booth arguing with a couple of technicians who kept shaking their heads. Finally Fred's voice came over a speaker: "You ready?"

"Yes," I said. "But there are only two cameramen here. I thought we'd use at least three cameras."

"Julia Child uses only two cameras," Fred said.

"In that case," I said, "I'm ready."

"Is your friend going to be on the set with you?" Fred asked. "We wouldn't want viewers confusing your show with 'The Incredible Hulk.'"

"Yeah, I'll need his assistance," I said.

"What'd he say?" Retch said.

"Nothing," I said.

"Okay, you're on!" Fred said.

I had no sooner gone into my introductory remarks than I detected a technical difficulty. The red light that indicates a television camera is on wasn't functioning on either camera. As soon as I had called Fred's attention to the problem, he corrected it, and I got my show under way again.

Looking back, I wish I hadn't tried quite so many complicated dishes on my first show. Otherwise, I don't think matters would have gotten out of hand.

I opened with my Whatcha-Got Hunters' Stew. As I explained, this stew derives its name from the situation of a group of hungry hunters meeting at night at the end of a mountain road and deciding to cook up a hearty meal before undertaking the long drive home.

"What we gonna cook?" one hunter will ask.

"How about a stew?" another hunter will say.

"What we gonna put in the stew?" still another hunter will inquire.

Then the hunter who suggested the stew will say, "Well, whatcha got?"

At that point the hunters will start rummaging around in their lunch sacks and food boxes and game pockets and trunks of their cars, tossing whatever they find into the stew pot. No one knows exactly what the ingredients of Whatcha-Got Hunters' Stew are because there is a firm rule against anyone shining a light onto it. I am told that once a hunter broke this rule and as a result had to be placed under a doctor's care for treatment of hypergagging.

Of course, I couldn't concoct an authentic Whatcha-Got Hunters' Stew in the television studio, but I came fairly close, or so I judged from the fact that when one of the cameramen zoomed in for a close-up shot of it he dropped to the floor, curled up in the prenatal position, and jammed a thumb in his mouth.

"One thing about camp cooking," my commentary went, "you can't be too picky about a few gnats, mosquitoes, ants, or even an occasional deerfly that happens to land in your stew. Since there are no live insects flying about the studio, ha, ha, I have to make do with some dried ones my kids gathered up for me in the garage. They are by no means as good as fresh insects but . . ."

At this point I was distracted by the sound of running footsteps headed for a restroom at the far end of the studio. I wondered in passing if television cameras can be operated by remote control, since cameramen seem to be such a temperamental lot. Still, there was nothing to do but continue with the show.

My Chipped Beef on a Shingle was a real smasheroo, judging from its impact on the individuals in the control booth.

My one moment of embarrassment came when I started to prepare Creek Mussels in Marshmallow Sauce and discovered that the piece of equipment on which I had placed the ingredients had heated up and the marshmallows had melted and dribbled down inside the thing. I was shocked, of course. You know how much marshmallows cost these days?

I had counted on Retch's assistance in the show, but early on a rather distinguished-looking lunatic in a pinstripe suit tried to rush onto the set. The guy probably would have ruined the whole show if Retch hadn't been able to get a half-nelson on him and wrestle him to the floor. There are some people who will do just about anything for a chance to clown around in front of a TV camera.

My most spectacular dish was the Flaming Bacon. It also provided me with the opportunity to demonstrate the proper procedure for extinguishing a small forest fire. I explained to the viewing audience that a shovel should always be carried for the purpose of smothering forest fires since one can't always expect to find the jacket of a pinstripe suit out in the woods.

Just as I was finishing up "The Camp Chef," my closing comments were practically drowned out by the sounds of sirens. As I told Retch while we were slipping out a back exit, you'd think television executives would wise up. Viewers are tired of all the violence on crime shows.

Several days later I happened to stumble across Fred as he was crawling under the front of my car with a hacksaw.

"Any idea when 'The Camp Chef' might be aired?" I asked him.

"Hoo hooo heeee haa hooo," he replied.

I could tell ol' Fred had been under a lot of strain

lately. That television business can really take it out of a person.

"Listen," I told him, "what you need is a good three-day fishing trip with me. Some of my camp cooking will straighten you out in nothing flat."

Oh, I tell you, the look of gratitude Fred gave me would have wrenched your heart!

The Heartbreak
of Astigmatism

☞ ☞ ☞When I was about fourteen the world turned fuzzy. I wasn't particularly concerned with the phenomenon at first, attributing it to the lateness of spring that year or possibly the Communists. It was a history teacher, Mrs. Axelrod, who finally diagnosed my affliction. She asked me to step to the front of the room and, with a long wooden pointer, indicate on the wall map the region occupied by Gaul. Not knowing Gaul from my left elbow, I decided to take a random stab at it anyway, since I figured the whole world, including the map, had become so blurred that no one would know the difference anyway. Also, my walk to the front of the classroom would give me an opportunity to display the attitude of debonair nonchalance I had been attempting to perfect. Arriving at the front of the room, I directed the pointer to a likely little fuzzy blotch. This drew a good laugh from the other kids, which I immediately capitalized on by doing a Gene Kelly soft-shoe routine on the way back to my desk.

"All right, Fred Astaire!" the teacher snarled. "I

want to see you dance yourself right back into this classroom immediately after school tonight!"

I was miffed. How could anyone mistake my Gene Kelly for a Fred Astaire? On the other hand, ever since the world had turned fuzzy, I myself was having trouble distinguishing the two of them even when they were forty feet high on the showhouse screen. Perhaps, I told myself, her *faux pas* was excusable.

I was hoping that by the time school was out, Mrs. Axelrod's rage would have withered a bit, but I found it still in full bloom. There was a rumor going around that the history teacher could kill flies in mid-air with her sarcasm, but I doubted there was any truth to it. Sure, a few flies may have been stunned but certainly not killed.

"Ah!" Mrs. Axelrod exclaimed as I entered the classroom. "The master of comic impersonations arrives!"

"Uh, I'm really sorry about that little dance," I apologized. "It was Gene Kelly, by the way."

"Oh, I should have known!" she replied. "I do hope you will forgive me!"

I flicked a stunned fly off my shoulder. "No problem," I said. "Anybody can make a mistake."

"Has anyone ever told you how obtuse you are?" she asked.

"No," I said, blushing, "but thank you very much. You're not so bad yourself, no matter what the kids say."

"Indeed!" she said, attempting to conceal her pleasure under a veil of wrath. "Well, now that the exchange of compliments is over, we are still left with the problem of Gaul."

"Actually," I confessed, "I didn't have the foggiest notion of where Gaul was, so I just took a flying guess. What country did I get?"

"Oh, you didn't get a country," she said with what I

thought I detected as a softening of tone. "You are apparently unaware that I also teach hygiene in this classroom. What you got was the bladder on an anatomical diagram of the human body!"

"Gee," I said, stunned. "It's a good thing you didn't ask me to point out Rome. We all would have been embarrassed."

"No doubt," she replied. "Are you by any chance having some trouble seeing clearly?"

"Not at all," I replied, gallantly scooping her folded coat up off her desk and helping her on with it. "Why do you ask?"

"Just a woman's intuition," she replied. "And little observations, such as the way you just now helped me on with the American flag."

"I did?" I said. "Well, to tell the truth, you look pretty good in stripes. Besides, it's so blurred that nobody would even guess it's a flag. Surely, you've noticed how fuzzy the world has become lately. I think it's the Communists doing it."

"My dear young man," she said. "I have some news for you. The world has not become fuzzy. Only *you* have become fuzzy. *You need glasses!*"

I was stunned. People had said a lot of bad things to me in my day, but this was the worst. I hadn't expected even Mrs. Axelrod to stoop this low, mean as she was. Didn't she know that I was famous for my vision, that my friends all called me Hawkeye. My gosh! Glasses! Spectacles! What was she saying? My mind reeled; my body beaded with sweat. If what Mrs. Axelrod said was true, that the world was not blurred, then my whole career was finished. No professional big-game guide could wear glasses! Jeez, could you imagine what one of my clients would think if I told him, "All right, we know the rhino's wounded and is going to charge as soon as we go in after him. But don't worry, I'm backing you up with my double-barreled elephant rifle. Before we start in, though, let me wipe the dust off my spectacles because I want to be able to see him real good."

And my squint! All the years I'd been practicing my squint, and now it was down the drain. A squint just doesn't look right behind a pair of glasses.

I tried to swear Mrs. Axelrod to secrecy, but she would have none of it. You probably have never met a person as mean as Mrs. Axelrod, so you may find it hard to believe the next thing she did. She called my parents and told them I needed glasses.

My folks wasted no time in hauling me down to an eye doctor to get me outfitted with spectacles. I did not go easily. My rage was such that it even worried the doctor. At one point he said to my mother, "Would you check his ropes again please? I think he's starting to work them loose."

Well, as I always said, you can buy a kid spectacles, but you can't make him wear them. I wore them only when my folks were around, and the rest of the time I carried them stuffed in my pocket where they stood a good chance of being broken. Then one day I was out in our pasture target practicing with my .22 rifle. After I had put ten successive shots right in the bull's-eye, the thought occurred to me that maybe if I wore my glasses I could hit a smaller bull's-eye, one less than three feet across. First, I made sure that no one was in the vicinity, a precaution I accomplished by shouting out "Hello! Anybody around!" Then I slipped the glasses out of my pocket and put them on.

The world snapped into focus. I could see mountains, trees, barns! I could see flowers and blades of grass and even ants crawling on the blades of grass. I hadn't seen ants in a year. I thought they had become extinct. It was . . . fantastic!

So after that whenever I went out into the great outdoors I wore my glasses, but only when alone. The real problem came when I was with the other guys. When we would go fishing, for example, I always had to pretend that I was clowning around.

"Hey, look at ol' Pat, he keeps casting his fly across the crick onto the sandbar! Ho, ho! That ol' Pat, he'll do anything for a laugh!" So then I'd have to go along with the gag and put on my hyena grin and wear my hat upside down. It was a real pain.

One day when my friend Peewee Thompson and I were sitting in my bedroom, I decided to sound him out on what he thought about people who wore glasses.

"Say, Peewee," I said. "You know that kid in the school band, Marvin Phelps, the one with the glasses, what do you think about the way he looks? He's a pretty good-looking kid, don't you think?"

Peewee gave me a nervous, sidelong glance. "I got to go home," he said.

"No, you idiot, what I mean is, do you think wearing glasses makes him look, uh, kinda funny?"

"Heck no. He's always worn glasses. He would look funny if he didn't wear them. He wouldn't even look like Four-Eyes Phelps if he didn't wear glasses. Why do you ask?"

"No reason," I said. "Just forget it."

"I'll tell you though," Peewee went on. "I sure wouldn't want ol' Four-Eyes Phelps backin' me up if I was goin' into the bush after a wounded rhino."

"I SAID FORGET IT!"

My greatest dread was that Rancid Crabtree would find out about my spectacles. If there was one thing

Rancid respected in another outdoorsman, it was keen vision. His own eyesight was superb. He was always the first to spot deer on a hunting trip. Pointing to a line of dots moving through the snow on the side of a mountain, he would say simply, "Deer." Then, while the rest of the hunters were straining to make out the dots, Rancid would say, "Mulies." The other hunters would stare at each other in disbelief. "Looks like they's all does, though. No, by gosh, one of 'em's a little spike buck!"

Rancid was the last person in the world I wanted to find out that I wore glasses. He wouldn't have any use for me after that.

One day we were in Rancid's old pickup truck on our way out to do some fishing, and, in his usual fashion, the old woodsman was pointing out distant sights to me. "Look up thar on thet side hill! Huncklebarries! Two or three of the little buggers are startin' to tarn color. Won't be long till they's ripe!"

I stared morosely off in the general direction he was pointing and tried to penetrate the green blur. "Yup. They sure do look like they're ripening up."

"Say, look at the size of them deer tracks crossin' the road. The deer thet made them was a biggun. Come fall, you 'n' me, we's gonna come up hyar an' look fer him, Ah kin tell you thet!"

"Yup," I said.

"What's wrong with you?" Rancid said. "You sound about as happy as a badger in a bees' nest."

"Nothin'," I said.

It was shortly after we got started fishing that Rancid began acting peculiar. Right at first he suggested that I fish upstream and he fish downstream.

"That's no fun," I told him. "We always fish together."

"Yeh," he said sheepishly. "Oh, all right, c'mon!"

The only good thing about my impaired vision was

that I could see perfectly up to a range of two feet. I therefore had no difficulty tying on the tiniest flies in my book, which I instantly deduced were the only flies likely to take trout in that particular time and place.

In the next twenty minutes or so I caught half a dozen fish. Rancid didn't get a single bite. "How come you don't change over to one of these little white flies?" I kept asking him. "That's what they're taking."

"Shoot," Rancid said. "Ah got this big ol' Grasshopper already tied on. Ah'll fish it."

Now this was totally unlike Rancid. I knew he didn't care all that much for work, but changing a fly didn't require any great effort. Usually he would have tried a dozen different flies by the time we got our feet wet. Then a whooper cutthroat (one that causes you to whoop, as distinguished from a mere whopper) smashed into my white fly. It took me a couple of minutes to land the fish.

"Wow, it's a beaut!" I whooped, thrashing my way across the creek to show Rancid the fish. When I was close enough, within two feet of him, I could see that his little eyes were bugged out in their comical fashion, as was their habit whenever he got excited.

"Gol-dang, thet's a purty fish!" he said, almost trembling. Instantly, he became stern. "You got any more of them itty-bitty white flies? All I brung with me was these big ones."

"Sure," I said, and handed him a couple.

Then Rancid did a remarkable thing. He reached into his pants pocket and hauled out a pair of spectacles, the kind you buy off the counter in a variety store. He put the glasses on, snipped the big fly off his tippet, and tied on the tiny one. Then he leveled a fierce glare at me.

"Wipe thet smirk off yer face," he snarled. "If you so much as open yer yap, I'll . . ."

I stepped back and thrust my hand into my pants pocket, took out my own glasses, and put them on. The stubby whiskers on Rancid's face snapped into focus. They quivered for a moment, then rippled out into the great crescent-shaped waves of his grin.

Neither one of us in all the years after that moment ever said a word about glasses. There was no need.

If a man like Rancid could wear glasses, I figured there couldn't be any shame in my wearing them. So the very next time I went out fishing with the guys, I showed up with my glasses on. The guys were all lifelong friends of mine, fellows I'd suffered with on a hundred camping trips. We had shared each other's triumphs and defeats, happiness and sorrows, the sweet and the bitter. When they saw me for the first time wearing my glasses, I learned once and for all the true meaning of friendship. It is that you don't thrash your friends within an inch of their lives if they laugh themselves silly when you show up wearing spectacles.

"What the heck," Peewee said later, after he had stopped pounding his thighs and had wiped away the tears of his mirth. "We ain't likely to run into a wounded rhino in this part of the country anyway."

Sneed

☞ ☞ ☞ **B**ack in the shadows of time when I was a youngster, a man by the name of Darcy Sneed lived in our county. I don't think I ever heard anyone say a kind word for Sneed, and I'm sure nobody ever heard me say one. He was always showing up without notice when and where he wasn't wanted and causing folks grief. Several times he scared the daylights out of me, catching me alone out in the woods, but except for one time I always managed to escape. As far as I know, Sneed never smiled nor cracked a joke. He was cold and hard and tight-lipped and generally unlikable. Besides that, he was the game warden.

Now, the truth is I seldom broke the game laws, not because I had any love for rules and regulations but because it seemed unsporting. Once, though, my friend Retch and I did sneak down to the creek early one morning three days before the opening of fishing season. We hid in some deep brush along the bank and at the first hint of dawn cast our salmon eggs out toward a logjam, where we knew some cutthroat had to be waiting. But I was so filled with dread and guilt that I couldn't enjoy fishing, and I knew that if I caught anything it would just compound the existing dread and guilt. Retch, on the other hand, didn't seem burdened by any doubts and was intently working his line so the eggs would drift under the logs. Somehow, I had to impress upon him that what we were doing was wrong. I searched for the right words, the kind of words that would convey to him the deep moral and ethical implications of our action. Then I thought of them.

"Sneed's comin'!" I hissed at him.

Retch instantly grasped the deep moral and ethical implications and reeled in his line so fast only its being wet saved it from instant combustion. We stashed our rods under a log and beat it out of there, hurrying down the creek trail. Retch was in front. As he rounded a bend, he turned his head slightly and said out of the corner of his mouth, "Good thing you seen him comin'."

"Who?" I said, already having forgotten the lie.

"Sneed," he said.

And there was Sneed, striding purposefully toward us down the trail.

"Howdy, Mr. Sneed," we said politely.

Sneed didn't say anything for a moment. He just let his glare rove over our quaking carcasses. The seconds passed, ticked off by the sound of our dripping sweat.

"What you boys doin' here?" he demanded finally.

We answered simultaneously: "Lookin' for a cow." "Pullin' up thistles."

Sneed didn't smile at these contradictory explanations. He was not a fun-loving man.

"I'm going to ask you boys one more time, what you *doin'* here?"

By now I had forgotten who had told him what, so I nudged Retch to go ahead and answer, he being the more experienced and polished liar. But Sneed's glare had penetrated Retch's brain and tangled his speech mechanism.

"We was just pullin' up cows," he said.

Sneed replied with another long silence. Then he said, "Let me see if I've got this straight. You two were down here on the crick at five in the morning pullin' up cows, is that correct?"

Right then I figured Sneed was going to throw us in jail, and for what? Not being able to think of a decent lie when we had to.

Sneed reached out and thumped a bony finger on Retch's chest. "I know and you know that you boys were down here fishin', gettin' a jump on the season. I'd arrest you both, but I didn't catch you at it. Next time I will."

Sneed knew how to put fear into a person. If he didn't manage to keep people from breaking the game laws, he at least kept them from enjoying it. He never forgot me after that morning on the creek, having filed me away in his memory bank as a person who took the game laws lightly and who bore watching.

Sneed was not one of those game wardens who come semi-attached to the seat of a pickup truck; he knew how to walk and was infamous for suddenly materializing in remote and roadless places. There was a friend of our family who was widely regarded as the best trapper in our part of the state. During the winter he would snowshoe far back into the high country to work his trap line. "It's real nice to be up there alone in the winter," he told me once. "There's just you and the silence and the snow and Sneed."

Numerous theories were set forth regarding the game warden. One was that there were actually three Sneeds. This was based on multiple sightings of Sneed in different parts of the county at the same time. Men would shake their heads and say, "There's something unnatural about Sneed."

One time I was sitting in the kitchen of a chronic poacher, and he told me how he had outsmarted Sneed once.

"I strapped my heels down on my snowshoes and walked backwards with the deer over my shoulder. Funniest thing you ever seen. I hid in some trees at the top of a rise to watch, and pretty soon Sneed hits my trail. He looks one way and t'other, and then he takes off followin' my tracks toward where I been." The poacher nearly split his sides laughing at the memory of his little trick.

His wife glared at him. "Now, Otis, you tell the boy the rest of the story, you hear?"

Otis sobered up and reluctantly finished the tale. "Well, when I got the deer back to my truck and started scrapin' the frost off the winders, there's ol' Sneed sittin' inside, smokin' a cigarette calm as you please."

"Cost us a hunnert dollars!" the wife snarled. "Ain't no deer worth no hunnert dollars!"

"Durn that Sneed," the poacher muttered, glowering into the coffee grounds at the bottom of his cup.

Another time, three men poached a deer close to the bottom of a rocky gorge and waited until after dark to sneak it up to their car parked on a road a half-mile up the mountain. The going was rough, and as they fought their way upwards over logs and rocks and through brush, one of the poachers plopped down on the ground for a rest and gasped, "Man, this is hard! It's a good thing there's four of us to drag this here deer, 'cause otherwise I don't think we'd make it."

One of the other poachers looked around, counting heads in the darkness. "Ain't *s'posed* to be but three of us draggin' this deer," he said nervously.

"Ain't s'posed to be nobody draggin' it!" Sneed said.

Over the years, I heard dozens of such tales about Sneed, some true, some imaginary, but their net effect was to leave me with the impression that the game warden was possessed of powers not generally found among the psychic accessories of ordinary human beings. I never went afield with rod or gun that I didn't feel Sneed's presence. One of my great fears was that I would sometime lose count and catch one fish over my limit, and Sneed would nab me. Then I'd be fined a hundred dollars and since neither my family nor I had ever seen a hundred dollars altogether at the same time, I would have to go to jail. Well, I wouldn't be able to stand being in jail, so I'd have to break out and steal a car and escape in a hail of gunfire. After that I'd probably kill a bank guard and be fatally wounded myself. And while I was sprawled on a sidewalk breathing my last, a reporter would come up to me and ask, "What made you do it, son?" And I'd tell him: "I caught one fish over my limit." It was easy to see how it all would work out, so anytime I got anywhere near my limit I practically wore my fish out counting them. It was a heavy burden for a kid, especially for one who didn't have any better grasp of mathematics than I did.

In the light of this background, it will be clear that my decision to fish the forbidden waters of the creek that fed the town reservoir was not arrived at casually. Despite all my fears and misgivings, I was simply overpowered by the logic that led me to the conclusion that that creek had to be crammed full of giant eastern brook. I should mention here that water pollution as such was unknown at the time. It was simply referred to then as "dumpin' stuff in the cricks." A few enlightened and farsighted individuals would occasionally speak out in the cause of pure water. "I wish folks would stop dumpin' stuff in the cricks," they would say, thereby branding themselves forever after as wild-eyed eccentrics. The only creek that was sacrosanct was that of the town reservoir, the townspeople being in unanimous agreement that they didn't want anyone dumping stuff in their drinking water. My reasoning, however, was this: (1) a dry fly wouldn't dirty the water; (2) I would be providing a civic service by removing trout that certainly had to be dirtying it; and finally (3) my family got its water out of a well. There was only one flaw in this logic: Sneed.

My plan of attack seemed foolproof, however. I would sneak into the reservoir under cover of predawn darkness, follow the creek up into the dense woods that would provide me cover through the day, then do my fishing and return after nightfall. I would carry a few carefully selected flies, a length of leader, and some line, and cut myself a willow pole when I reached the spot where I wanted to start fishing. The night before I launched my assault on Reservoir Creek, I went to bed early, chuckling evilly over the boldness of the plan, beautiful even in its very simplicity. Ol' Sneed, as I told myself, had finally met his match.

Thus it was that I found myself returning home late the following evening with a fine catch of brook trout. The fishing had been just as fantastic as I had known it would be. Nevertheless, I was filled with fear and remorse and a dark sense of foreboding about what the future held for me. Part of the reason for these feelings was that I knew I had deliberately and maliciously broken the law, discovering too late that I possessed neither the temperament nor the taste for crime. The rest of the reason was that I was sitting alongside of Sneed in the front seat of his dusty old Dodge sedan.

As I had come sneaking up over the edge of a logging road on my way out of the reservoir basin, there was Sneed, sitting in his car with the lights off. True to his fashion, he didn't say a word. He just leaned over, pushed open the door on the passenger side, and motioned for me to get in. For an instant I thought of running, but then decided against it. You just can't move all that fast when you're paralyzed.

While Sneed drove along in his usual silence, I tried to appeal to his sympathy, even though from all the reports I'd heard no one had ever detected a smidgen of it in him.

"Look, Mr. Sneed," I said, "maybe it don't matter none to you, sending a kid to jail, but don't you care nothin' about that poor bank guard? What's his little children gonna do without him?"

"What bank guard?" Sneed said.

Before I could explain, a voice from the back seat said, "Ain't no use pleadin' with him, boy. When he was born, they heated him white hot and tempered him in oil, and he's been hard ever since."

This dismal report had issued from a tall, lean young man sprawled across the back seat and chewing on a match. He was covered with dirt and bits of grass and brush, apparently acquired in an attempt to escape from Sneed.

"What did he get you for?" I asked my fellow criminal, feeling an instant kinship with him.

"Nothin' a-tall. I was just up there on the mountain tryin' out my new jacklight. It must have riled up this ol' buck deer, 'cause first thing I know he come chargin' at me out of the brush. I had to shoot him to save my life!"

"Shut up, LeRoy," Sneed said. "You can tell it all to the judge."

About that time we drove up in front of my house. Sneed stopped the car and motioned for me to get out.

"You mean you ain't arresting me?" I said.

"What for?" Sneed said. "It ain't my responsibility to keep folks from fishin' that reservoir; it's the Water Department's. They own the water, and they own the fish in it. Besides, I get my drinkin' water from a well."

The game warden went on to tell me, in his tone of cold certainty, that he would turn me over to the Water Department for appropriate punishment if he ever caught me within a mile of the reservoir again. I nodded solemnly, even though inside I was chuckling silently to myself. Ol' Sneed did have a soft spot after all, and I, with my boyish charm, had touched it. No doubt I had reminded him of his own son or perhaps even of himself as a boy. Even before the sound of Sneed's old Dodge had faded off in the distance, my resolve to retire from a life of crime had vanished and I was already plotting my next raid on the reservoir. Even if he did catch me, I knew the game warden wouldn't have the heart to turn me in to the Water Department.

What changed my mind was an item my grandmother read in the newspaper the following week.

"I see by the paper where a fellow by the name of LeRoy Sneed was fined a hundred dollars for poaching deer," she said. "When are folks ever gonna learn to obey the law?"

One folk learned right then, and I'm happy to report that I've never intentionally violated so much as a single game regulation since. Oh, I've been tempted several times, but even though Sneed has been dead for fifteen years now, you just never can tell about a man like that.

The Hunter's Dictionary

☞ ☞ ☞**M**any persons who have just started hunting mistakenly assume that they understand the specialized terminology and jargon of the sport. As a result, they spend years in a state of befuddlement, wondering at the perversity of fate and cursing the contrariness of experienced hunters.

The problem is that they simply don't grasp the true meaning of the terms, phrases, and casual utterances as used by the hunting fraternity. I have therefore compiled *The Hunter's Dictionary*, published below in its entirety. It will do nothing to improve the beginning hunter's skills but should go a long way toward preserving his mental health.

It has long seemed to me to be an affectation of the overeducated to insist that dictionaries be printed in alphabetical order. If during my years spent in first grade I had succeeded in learning the alphabet, I might now feel more kindly toward it. In fact, I am rather fond of that portion of it that runs up to the letter *G*; beyond that point my feeling is largely one of hostility. So much for the explanation of why this dictionary is presented in a random and, to my mind, more meaningful order.

One further note: For the purpose of conciseness, "beginning hunter" and "experienced hunter" are abbreviated "BH" and "EH," respectively.

Without further display of my mastery of lexicography, I herewith present *The Hunter's Dictionary.*

FIVE MINUTES—This refers to a period of time ranging from five minutes to eight hours, generally speaking, but has been known to run as long as five days. It is used in this way: "Wait here. I'll be back in five minutes." What happens is that the EH who makes the statement will step off into the brush to check for tracks or possibly for some other business. While there, he will catch sight of a deer fifty yards or so up the slope, but the deer's head will be behind a tree. The hunter crouches down and sneaks up to a little rise off to one side to get a better look and determine the sex of the deer. It turns out to be a nice buck, which is just stepping over the ridge of the hill. The hunter, still in his crouch, scurries silently up the hill, expecting an easy shot. Cresting the hill, he catches a glimpse of its tail as the deer rounds the bend of an old logging road. The hunter will be occupied with this pursuit for the next few hours. His companion, if he too is an EH, will wait no longer than it takes to consume half a sandwich and a cup of coffee. By then he knows that the "five minutes" is a period to be measured in hours, and he will immediately proceed with his own hunting. A BH, on the other hand, assuming that "five minutes" means five minutes, will remain rooted loyally to the waiting place until lichens begin to form on him. When the EH finally returns, the lichen-covered hunter will yell at him, "I thought you said you'd be back in five minutes!"

The EH, somewhat puzzled by this display of wrath, will glance at his watch and say, "Well, here I am, ain't I? I left at ten-thirty, and now it's only five-fifteen! If I was going to be gone longer than five minutes, I would've told you!"

HUNTING VEHICLE—The BH assumes that what is meant by this phrase is any vehicle used to transport persons on a hunting trip, preferably a four-wheel drive of some sort. What the EH means by a "hunting vehicle" is *any* vehicle so long as it isn't his. If a BH is along on the trip, it means the BH's vehicle specifically. It matters not that the EH owns an outfit capable of swimming rivers and climbing trees or that the BH owns a sports car. The EH will merely glance at the sports car and observe: "Nice little hunting rig you have here."

FUNNY NOISE—A sound the EH reports the engine of his vehicle to be making any time the subject arises as to whose rig should be used for the hunting trip.

IMPASSABLE ROAD—Any road that gives indications it might mar the paint job or muddy the hub caps, provided the vehicle under consideration belongs to the EH.

PRACTICALLY A FOUR-LANE HIGHWAY—Any terrain slightly less hazardous than a streambed at flood stage, provided the vehicle under consideration does not belong to the EH.

BUILT TO TAKE IT—Describes any hunting vehicle not the EH's.

OOOOOOOOEEEEE-AH-AH-AH!—If there's one thing I hate, it's putting on cold, wet pants in the morning!

PNEUMONIA—What the EH claims to have whenever it's his turn to climb out of a warm sleeping bag and build the morning fire. Between spasms of hideous coughing, the EH may also request that someone say some kind words over his remains if he drops dead while returning from starting the fire.

MIRACULOUS RECOVERY—What the EH experiences as soon as he hears the morning fire crackling cheerily and smells coffee perking and bacon frying.

CAMP COOK—The guy who draws the short straw.

OVERDONE—Used by camp cooks to mean "burnt to a crisp."

BURNED—At some point the meal was totally engulfed by flames. The meal is still regarded as edible provided the hunting trip has been under way for at least three days.

RARE—The wood was too wet to start a cooking fire.

HASH—What all hunting-trip breakfasts appear to be. There is yellow hash, brown hash, gray hash, black hash, and green hash. Only a fool eats green hash.

STEW—Basically the same as green hash.

BLEEPING BLEEP-OF-A-BLEEP!—Phrase used by EH to announce he has just stepped out of a boat three feet short of the duck blind in the darkness of a cold December morning.

IMPOSSIBLE SHOT—What the EH has made anytime he downs game farther away than fifty feet.

FAIR SHOT—Any impossible shot made by someone other than the EH.

DID YOU FEEL THAT EARTH TREMOR JUST NOW?—Question asked by EH immediately after missing an easy shot.

A BIT—A lot.

SOME—All. As in, "I ate some of those little cheese-flavored crackers you had hidden in the bottom of your pack."

LEG CRAMP—What the EH insists is killing him and which requires that he get out of the hunting vehicle and "walk it out" on any occasion that a treacherous stretch of road appears up ahead.

TO MAKE A LONG STORY SHORT—The EH is about to

relate a story approximately the length of the history of mankind since the Creation.

I'M ABSOLUTELY CERTAIN THIS IS THE RIGHT TURN—There's one chance in ten this is the right turn.

IT AIN'T GONNA RAIN—Pitch tent on high ground and begin work immediately on a log raft.

AAAIIII!—The hash has become too hot for the camp cook's stirring finger.

BAFF MAST PIME IG BEAD FEAS MID MIFF PIFE!—That's the last time I try to eat peas in the dark with my hunting knife!

WHAT'S THAT? DID YOU HEAR SOMETHING PROWLING AROUND OUTSIDE THE TENT JUST NOW?—Questions hissed to arouse snoring tent partner and keep him awake for the rest of the night, listening.

DEER STAND—What the BH is placed on to keep him out of the way of the EH.

JAMMED RIFLE, DAMAGED GUNSIGHT, BLINDING HEADACHE, BAD KNEE, FOGGED SPECTACLES, ACUTE IRREGULARITY, SPONTANEOUS REGULARITY, and GREEN HASH—Any one or all of these are given as reasons the BH got a deer and the EH didn't.

CONSUMMATE SKILL—Why the EH got a deer and the BH didn't.

MEETING PLACE—An imaginary point in space that hunters are supposed to converge upon at a particular time. It is sometimes referred to as The Big Snag, The Old Apple Orchard, The Car, and Camp. The EH knows that such a place is merely a figment of the imagination and that the proposed meeting will never occur. It is hard for an EH to keep a straight face whenever a meeting place is spoken of.

A TRUE STORY—A collection of the most outrageous, preposterous, and unmitigated lies ever assembled.

DRESSED OUT AT 140 POUNDS—Dressed out at eighty pounds.

A RUNNING SHOT AT OVER 200 YARDS—I don't know how those powder burns got on its hide.

FLAT TRAJECTORY—Describes the movement of a hunter leaving his sleeping bag one hour after having eaten green hash for supper.

DID ANYONE THINK TO BRING—I left it sitting on my kitchen table.

MY CARDIOLOGIST—A mythical person casually referred to by the EH whenever it is suggested that he help haul a dead elk up the side of a steep mountain.

A HUNTING TIP—What the EH pays his hunting guide to keep his mouth shut and not to regale the boys back at the camp with an amusing account of what happened.

LEAVE THE LANTERN ON; IT'LL ATTRACT THE INSECTS AND KEEP THEM OFF OF US—I have trouble getting to sleep without a night light.

I SCOUTED OUT A LOT OF REAL NICE COUNTRY ON THE OTHER SIDE OF THE MOUNTAIN—The EH was lost for most of the day.

DON'T WORRY—Worry.

WIND, SNOW, COLD; THIS IS THE MOST MISERABLE DAY I'VE SPENT IN MY LIFE—Had a great time.

NEXT TIME, KID, TRY NOT TO MAKE SO MUCH RACKET, TROMPING THROUGH THE BRUSH THE WAY YOU DO. BOY, I'VE NEVER SEEN SUCH A CASE OF BUCK FEVER AS THAT ONE OF YOURS! ALSO, YOU'VE GOT TO LEARN NOT TO SHOUT, "THERE'S A BUCK!" JUST AS I'M SETTIN' THE CROSS HAIRS ON HIM. HA! AND THOSE TRACKS YOU THOUGHT WERE FRESH? WHY, YOU COULD HAVE GATHERED THEM UP AND SOLD THEM TO A MUSEUM AS FOSSILS! GEEZ!—You did all right, kid.

Tenner
Shoes

☞ ☞ ☞ "**W**hy don't you throw out some of these shoes?" my wife shouted from inside the closet.

"Are you crazy, woman?" I replied. "I *need* all those shoes—my bowling shoes, my jogging shoes, my hiking shoes, my canoeing shoes, my sailing shoes, my black dress shoes, my brown dress shoes, my brown casual shoes, my black casual shoes, my white casual shoes, my moccasins, my hip boots, my waders, my canvas wading shoes, my hunting boots, my mountain-climbing boots, my down booties, my camp shoes, my sandals, my . . ."

"Stop! Stop!" my wife screamed. "I give up! You can keep them! What I wish, though, is that somebody would invent a pair of shoes that could be used for everything."

Well, as a matter of fact, somebody once did. I wore them every summer when I was a kid. The shoe's inventor, I believe, was a Mr. Tenner. At least that's what we called them—Tenner shoes.

Once a rich kid moved to our town and tried to tell us that the shoes we were wearing were not called Tenner shoes at all but tennis shoes. We'd never seen anyone as ignorant as that kid. He didn't even wear Tenner shoes, so we wondered why he thought he knew so much about them.

"You tryin' to tell us these shoes weren't invented by a Mr. Tenner?" Retch Sweeney said to the kid. "How come everybody calls them Tenner shoes, then?"

"Only illiterates call them Tenner shoes," the kid shot back. Naturally, that got us all riled up, and we started yelling at him and pushing him and trying to get him to fight one of us.

"Listen," Peewee Thompson said. "We're all just as normal as you are, except for maybe Birdy—he's a little weird."

"No, no!" the rich kid shouted. "'Illiterate' means you don't know how to read and write." Well, as soon as we found out that we hadn't been insulted, everybody cooled down and started patting the kid on the back and telling him he was all right after all, and we hoped he wouldn't harbor any hard feelings against us because of a little misunderstanding.

"Just the same," Retch said, "I ain't never heard of anybody by the name of Tennis."

"I did once," I said. "I think his son was one of them English poets, but I doubt either one of them knew anything about shoes."

Tenner shoes were made out of black canvas and had rubber soles and little round patches over the part that covered your anklebones. They were ugly. Tenner designed them that way on purpose so girls wouldn't want to wear them.

You got your pair of Tenner shoes each spring about the time the snow began to recede from the lowlands. There was an interesting little ritual that went with the purchase of each year's Tenner shoes. My mother would take me down to Hobbs's dry goods store, where Mr. Hobbs himself waited on the shoe customers.

"Howdy," Mr. Hobbs would say. "By golly, I bet you brought that young colt in to get him shod." Mr. Hobbs and my mother would cackle at monotonous length over this witticism. Interestingly enough, when I was very young and first heard the little joke, I thought Hobbs had said, "to get him shot." My fright was such that I behaved myself for the better part of the day and wondered long afterwards in what manner my sentence had been commuted.

Hobbs's arsenal of wit seemed to consist of the single joke, and as soon as he had spent that round on his customers he seemed to revert immediately into his natural self, perhaps best described as peevish.

"Siddown and take off your shoes," he would order. The shoes he referred to were generally some kind of clodhopper boots well along into the first stage of oblivion, heels and tongue missing, soles flopping loose, seams gaping, the laces a Chinese puzzle of knots and frayed ends. As I peeled off the boots, Mr. Hobbs and my mother would both leap back and gasp.

"I thought I told you to wash your feet!" my mother would screech, more for Mr. Hobbs's benefit than my own. "I've never seen the likes of it."

Mr. Hobbs would mutter under his breath about having seen the likes of it, something about hygiene films in Navy boot camp.

"How's that?" my mother would say.

"Nothing," Mr. Hobbs would snort. "Nothing."

He would then lock one of my feet in a measuring device, all the while doing his impression of a person removing a long-dead rat from a trap. The measurement taken, Hobbs would get up and return shortly with a box of Tenner shoes, which he would drop in my lap and order me to try on.

Even to this day I recall with ecstasy the pure sensual delight of slipping my feet into a brand-new pair of Tenner shoes, my ol' toes up in the forward part wiggling around, checking out their new quarters, the ankles swelling boastfully under the protective cushions of the rubber patches as the fat clean laces snugged tight the embrace of canvas and rubber. After a winter of wearing the clodhopper boots, I felt like I was strapping on a pair of wings.

"I better go try them out," I would say.

"Stay in the store!" Mr. Hobbs would shout. "Don't take them out of the store!"

But it would be too late. I would be out on the sidewalk, and the Tenner shoes would be carrying me in free soaring flight around the block. The test completed, I would brake to a screeching stop and reenter the store.

"Maybe just a half-size larger," I would tell Mr. Hobbs. "Gosh, I don't know why anyone would let their dog run loose on the sidewalk, but I washed these Tenner shoes off good as new in a mud puddle and as soon as they dry . . ."

"Dog?" Mr. Hobbs would say. *"Dog!* Nothing doing! Those are your size! That'll be ninety-eight cents, Missus."

"Ninety-eight cents!" my mother would say. "My land, I don't know what folks are going to do if prices keep going up the way they are."

"Terrible," Mr. Hobbs would mutter. "Don't know these young whelps are worth it anyways." He always sounded as if he meant it, too.

To my mind, the Tenner was the ultimate shoe. You could use it for running and hiking and jumping, for playing football and basketball, hunting and fishing, mountain climbing, rafting, spelunking, swimming, bicycling, horseback riding, cowback riding, pigback riding. Whatever the activity, the Tenner shoe adapted itself to the task in noble and admirable fashion.

The one area in which the Tenner shoe may have fallen a bit short was as a dress-up shoe. Suppose, for example, that you had to go to some social event where all the youngsters were dressed up in their best clothes. You showed up wearing your good pair of pants, your good shirt, your good socks, and your Tenner shoes, which by now may have been showing the strain of hunting, fishing, pigback riding, etc. Now, as soon as you got within hearing distance of some of the other mothers at the affair, your mother would look down at your feet, conjure up an expression of absolute horror, and say, "I thought I told you to wear *your brown oxfords!* My land, you'll mortify me to death! Just look at those filthy old Tenner shoes."

Now of course all of the other mothers would look at your mother and smile and shake their heads in an understanding way as if to say, "What can you expect of little boys?" What was truly shrewd about this charade was your mother's use of the phrase "your brown oxfords." This not only implied that you *had* brown oxfords but also black ones and possibly white ones. Maybe one of the reasons the ruse worked so well was that most of the other guys had protruding from the cuffs of their good pairs of pants the unmistakable rubber noses of Tenner shoes. If there was a poor kid present at one of these social functions, by the way, his mother would look down at his feet and say, "Land sakes, Henry, didn't I tell you to wear shoes!" Of course, all of us guys knew that Henry didn't have any shoes. Otherwise, why would he paint his feet to look as if he were wearing Tenners? It made you kind of sad if you thought about it.

The great thing about Tenners was their almost unlimited versatility. They were great for wearing inside a sleeping bag, for example. Nowadays, of course, there are little down booties especially designed for wearing inside of sleeping bags. The one problem with these booties is that they really aren't designed for outside wear, and if you have to get up in the night for any reason, they're not much good for wandering around over rough ground in the dark. Of course, when you're camping out as a kid, there is only one thing that can make you get up in the middle of the night, and that is the necessity of running for your life. And if ever there was a shoe designed for running for your life, it was the Tenner. Many was the dark night that a troop of us young campers made our way home, trailing in our wake the distinct odor of smoldering Tenners.

Tenners made great fishing waders. Mr. Tenner, who must have been an absolute genius, had designed them without any insulation so that when you waded out into an icy spring stream it took only a few minutes for your feet to turn numb. From then on you could fish in complete comfort. The numbness also prevented you from feeling any pain when your Tenners slithered into narrow and odd-shaped openings between slippery rocks. You could continue fishing in blissful comfort up above while down below the rocks committed various acts of depravity on your feet, rearranging the bones in imaginative ways, doing trick shuffles with your toes, and playing football with your ankles. We would often return from a fishing trip with an affliction known technically as cauliflower feet. Fortunately, we had the good sense never to remove our Tenners until they had dried, thereby preserving our feet in the shape, if not exactly of feet, at least of Tenners. Indeed, I was often afraid to remove my Tenners after a fishing trip for fear of what I might find inside them. I have always had a weak stomach.

There was considerable controversy among us about how often Tenners should be taken off. The conservatives argued for once a week, the liberals for three or four times a summer, and the radicals for never, preferring to allow decay and disintegration to take their natural course. Although I was one of the conservatives, I shared the radicals' curiosity over whether, when their Tenners finally self-destructed, there would be any feet left inside.

I frequently shared space in small tents with Tenner radicals, and the idea occurred to me more than once to take a caged canary in with me so that its sudden demise could warn me when the gas escaping from the radicals' Tenners had reached a lethal level. To my knowledge, there were never any human fatalities from this cause, although large numbers of flying and crawling insects in the tent died mysteriously.

There were many other theories concerning the proper use of Tenner shoes. These theories were passed on from the older fellows to the younger ones and were usually taken at face value. One of these theories was passed on to me by my cousin Buck, several years my senior, who told me that little slits should be cut in the canvas of new Tenner shoes so that in an emergency you could thrust some of your toes out through the slits and get better traction. This seemed to me to be a good idea, even though I could never bring myself to cut a brand-new pair of Tenners. It was just as well. In fact, I'll never forget the day I saw this theory put to the test.

Buck had taken me on a little hiking trip in the

mountains for the purpose of instructing me in wood-craft. He was one of those people who loved to teach but can never be bothered learning anything. What Buck taught me was any odd thought that happened to pop into his head, and some of the thoughts were pretty odd. He taught me, for example, that woodpeckers were tapping out code on the trunks of dead trees, warning other woodpeckers of our approach. He even let me in on the secret that he had cracked this code and knew what they were saying. Sometimes, he said, the wood-peckers even made jokes in code, and Buck had to laugh when he heard them.

"What did that one say?" I would ask Buck when he laughed.

"Oh, you're too little for me to repeat a joke like that to," he would say. "But I can tell you this—them woodpeckers is pretty funny birds!"

It turned out that Buck's theory about slitting Tenners to stick your toes out of was on a par with his knowledge of ornithology. After what happened that day on the mountain, I never again had any use for Buck's teachings. What happened was this: We were walking along single file, with Buck, of course, in the lead, reciting all sorts of incredible nature lore to me. The weather was chilly and the earth on the mountain frozen hard, with patches of snow still lingering here and there. As we were making our way down the unexplored back side of the mountain, we came to a huge slab of rock approximately fifty feet square and slanting down to a drop-off. The surface of the rock was smooth and covered with frost. Buck started walking straight across the rock. I stopped.

"Whatcha stop for?" Buck asked, turning around about halfway across the slab. "Tenner shoes don't slide on rock. The little suction cups on the soles, they grab right onto the . . ."

Buck was sliding.

"Well, this frost makes it a little slick," he said. "I better . . ."

By now Buck was *really* sliding. He gave up all efforts at further conversation and devoted his full attention to scrambling back up the rock. The problem was that no matter how fast and furious Buck's scramble was, his downward rate of slide seemed to be greater by about an inch per second. I had no idea how much of a drop awaited him at the brink of the slab—a hundred feet, half a mile? I remembered all the mountain-climbing movies I'd ever seen where a climber loses his grip and plummets downward until he is just a tiny, noisy speck hurtling toward the patchwork farmlands below. From the look on his face, I knew Buck was remembering the same movies. Then I noticed that Buck had forgotten to stick his toes out through the slits in his Tenners.

"Stick out your toes, Buck," I screamed at him. "Stick out your toes!"

Buck's toes suddenly emerged from the slits like little pink landing gear, and I have to admit that he did some marvelous things with his toes—in fact, just about everything it is possible to do with toes and not get arrested. But nothing worked.

Buck shot backward right off over the edge of the cliff. His drop was accompanied by a long, horrible, slowly diminishing scream.

I was a bit puzzled by the scream, since Buck was standing there on a wide ledge just three feet down from the brink of the slab, his whole top half still in full view of me. Later, he tried to tell me he was just doing his imitation of Tarzan's ape call. Well, I'd heard his imitation of Tarzan's ape call numerous times, and it had never before made my hair stand on end. Buck was finished as a mentor. I was just happy that I hadn't followed his advice and violated a perfectly good pair of Tenners by cutting slits in them for an emergency.

As with all good things, Tenners did not last forever. Spring eased into summer and summer wore on, and the Tenners would begin to fade, the dark rich black of the canvas turning to pale dirty gray. Then the seams where the rubber was glued to the canvas would start to peel loose. The eyelets for the laces would begin popping out. The laces themselves would break and have to be knotted; their ends would fray out into tiny pompoms. The round rubber ankle patches would fall off. The canvas at the balls of the feet would wear through. Then a tear would move back along the instep. By September the Tenners would be done for.

On the first day of school, your new clodhopper boots felt good. Their weight gave you a sense of security, of substance, of manhood, and the will to face another year of school. But there would be a note of sadness, too, because Henry, the poor kid, would be there, his feet painted to look like new boots. You tried not to think about it.

My wife's muffled voice came from inside the closet. "How about this pair of shoes? Can I at least give these to the Salvation Army?"

"Those old tennis shoes? Sure, go ahead," I said. "Hell, I never play tennis, anyway."

Reading Sign

☞ ☞ ☞ **B**ack when I was a kid, the mark of a true woodsman was his ability to read sign. Knowing this, many persons trying to pass themselves off as woodsmen would make a great show of staring at sign for a few minutes and then offering up profound remarks about it:

"I'd judge from this broken twig that we're about ten minutes behind a herd of mule deer, most of them yearlings or does, but there's one big fella I'd guess to be a trophy buck. You'll know him when you see him 'cause he favors his left front leg when he's running flat out and . . ."

The only way to deal with a person like that was to walk over, look down, and say, "For heaven's sake, so that's where I dropped my lucky twig! The amazing thing is, I broke it three months ago and it still works!" You then picked up the twig, put it in your pocket, and strolled away.

My cousin Buck was one of these impostors. Even though I was several years younger than Buck, sign was

150

serious business to me and I spent long hours reading about it and studying it first-hand and trying to find out what it meant and whether it was sign at all or maybe just an accident. Buck, on the other hand, couldn't concentrate on any subject longer than fifteen seconds unless it wore a dress and smelled of perfume, which sign seldom if ever did. Still, ever so often I had to endure his hauling me out to the woods to instruct me on how to read sign.

"Hey, looky here," he would hiss at me. "Elk sign!"

Now, any fool could see that the sign was not that of an elk but the handiwork of a mule who stood nearby with a smile on his face and a snicker in his voice. If I hadn't been smarter than I looked, I would have pointed that fact out to Buck. But not wishing to have my head thumped, I said, "Yes! Elk! Elk! I can see now they were elk!"

Thumping your head was Buck's way of proving to you that he could read sign.

If I, on the other hand, happened to discover some fresh deer sign, Buck would always dismiss my find with a shrug of his shoulders and the profound bit of wisdom: "You can't eat sign."

He lived to regurgitate those words.

One frosty November morn Buck had dragged me out deer hunting with him. I wasn't old enough yet to carry a rifle, but Buck needed someone along to brag to about how he could read sign. We were cruising down a back road in Buck's old car, listening to Gene Autry on the radio and looking for deer. (Buck believed the way to hunt deer was to drive up and down roads; that's the sort of woodsman he was.) For breakfast I had brought along some chocolate-covered peanuts in my jacket pocket, and ever so often I'd sneak one into my mouth so Buck wouldn't see it and demand a share. There was some fool notion in those days that if someone saw you with something good to eat, all he had to do was yell "divvies" at you and then you had to share with him. If you didn't share with somebody when he yelled "divvies" at you, he got to beat you up and take it all—but only if he was bigger than you were. If he was smaller, he could yell "divvies" till the sun went down and you didn't have to share with him. In that way, I suppose, it was an equitable system. But I digress.

So anyway, there we were driving down the back road, and all at once Buck hit the brakes and yelled out, "Deer tracks!" Sure enough, even from where I now sat, wedged up under the dashboard, I could see that sometime during the past six months a deer had come sliding and bounding through the soft dirt of a high bank above the road. As soon as the car had slid to a stop, we jumped out, Buck breathlessly thumbing cartridges into his rifle, and rushed over to examine the tracks. All the while, Buck was making sure he got full credit for spotting the tracks.

"I told you they was deer tracks, and you didn't believe me, did you?" he whispered, his voice shrill with excitement.

"I believed you, Buck."

"Hell, we musta been drivin' past fifty miles an hour and I looks out and I says to you, 'There's some deer tracks!' Now didn't I say that?"

"That's what you said, Buck."

We looked at the tracks. Buck got down on his knees and felt the edges of the tracks, apparently to see if they were still warm. Then he bent over and sniffed them! It was almost too much to bear for a serious student of deer tracks. Any fool could see those tracks were so old they could have been classified as fossils. The deer who made them no doubt had since known a long and happy life and finally expired at a ripe old age.

"They fresh, Buck?" I asked.

Buck stood up and tugged at his wispy beard as he studied the tracks. "I'd say he went through here, oh, about a half-hour before daylight."

"Gee," I said, stifling a yawn. "We just missed him, hunh? Dang. If we had just been a few minutes earlier, hunh, Buck?"

"Yep," Buck said. "Well, win some, lose some."

While I was racking my brain trying to think of some that Buck had won, a terrible idea occurred to me. And the instant the idea occurred, I implemented it. Even after thirty years and more I am still ashamed of pulling it on Buck. That I am still convulsed with laughter upon recalling the expression on his face is even more despicable. Only the desire to ease my conscience compels me to confess the deed. What I did—oh, I shudder still to think of it—was to take a handful of the chocolate-covered peanuts and sprinkle them on the ground by my feet.

"Hey, Buck," I said, pointing. "Sign. Looks fresh, too."

Buck looked at me in disgust and shook his shaggy head. "How many times I got to tell ya: Ya can't eat sign!"

At that, I reached down, picked up a chocolate-covered peanut, snapped it into the air, and caught it in my mouth.

Buck's jaw dropped halfway to his belt buckle.

For years afterwards, Buck couldn't stand the sight of chocolate-covered peanuts. Offer him one and his upper lip would flutter like a broken window shade. Sure, when ol' Buck figured out the trick I'd played on him, he thumped my head until both of us were worn out, but that didn't change the obvious truth: He just wasn't a proper woodsman.

Much of my early knowledge about sign was gained

from reading books and magazine articles. These usually included drawings of the tracks of various wild animals, and all you had to do was memorize the shape and the number of toes and so on to be able to identify the track out in the wilds. I spent endless hours at this sort of study, but it was well worth the effort. For one thing, it taught me about true friendship. If you were out with one of your friends in the woods, you could point to a set of tracks and say, "Look, lynx tracks."

"Gee," the friend would say in a properly apprecia- tive tone. If he didn't say that or an equivalent expres- sion, he wasn't your friend.

Now, if you followed the lynx tracks and at the other end of them found a skunk waddling along, you would say to your friend, studying him closely, "Sometimes skunks make lynx tracks, did you know that?"

"No, I didn't," he might reply. "That's really in- teresting." Such a reply could mean only two things: This guy was impossibly stupid, or he was a *really* good friend.

Strangely enough, many of the magazine articles on sign were written by a lady. Her underlying principle was that wild animals were actors on the stage of the great outdoors. If you could read the scripts, namely their tracks in the snow, you could decipher the plot. A typical plot would go like this: Rabbit tracks are crossing the snow from one direction and coyote tracks from another. The two sets of tracks intersect at the base of a tree. Only the coyote tracks continue on from the tree. Hmmmmmmmmmmmm. How did the the rabbit get away from the tree without making any tracks? Did he climb the tree? The mystery was almost mind-boggling. The author of these articles could take an hour's walk through the snow and encounter a dozen fascinating little dramas, none of which, I might add, were ever comedies.

I hate to admit it, but at a certain age I was intrigued by these articles and was forever searching the snowy countryside for evidence of little wildlife dramas. Unfortunately, most of the dramas I encountered went about like this: Rabbit tracks emerge from thicket, go under barbwire fence, mess around in a patch of blackberry brambles, cross a creek over thin ice, go under another barbwire fence, mosey back across the thin ice, meander through the blackberry brambles again, pass under another barbwire fence, and go back into the thicket. That would be it. Although the drama itself might be deadly dull, following the "script" around the countryside could be fraught with pain, danger, and excitement. Several times I nearly froze to death in my wet clothes while rushing home to bandage my scratches and cuts and to dig out the stickers.

Where I really learned to read sign was from the old woodsman Rancid Crabtree. Rancid didn't care a hoot about reading little woodland dramas. To him, sign was not a form of entertainment but an essential element in a complex scheme that he had devised to make working for a living unnecessary. About the only things Rancid needed money for were a few clothes, rifle and shotgun shells, salt and pepper, some gas for his old truck, chewin' tobacco, and his medicine, which a local pharmacist, a Colt .45 stuffed in the waistband of his pants, delivered at night in quart-sized Mason jars. These commodities required cash, particularly the medicine. Rancid acquired his cash by running a little trap line each winter. And successful trapping required a rather extensive knowledge of sign. The intensity and seriousness with which Rancid studied sign can be fully appreciated only by realizing that to him it was virtually the same thing as tobacco and medicine. To Rancid, sign was a matter of ultimate concern.

A stroll with Rancid through the woods was a course in post-graduate study in reading sign. "B'ar," he would say, pointing to the ground as we walked along. "Porky-pine . . . bobcat . . . skonk . . ." And so on. One day we were going along in this fashion and he pointed down and said, "Snake."

"Snake?" I said to myself, glancing down. "This is a new . . . SNAKE!" My bare foot was descending toward the fat, frantic reptile. Despite my precarious posture, I managed to execute a successful lift-off before coming into actual contact with the creature. While involved in this effort, I left my vocal cords unattended and they took advantage of their moment of freedom to get off a loud and startling shriek. Upon hearing this, Rancid leaped to the conclusion that he had misjudged the snake as being a member of a benevolent sect and immediately began to curse and hop about and flail the earth with his walking stick. It was all pretty exciting, and Rancid was more than a little annoyed when he found out the snake hadn't taken a bite out of me after all.

"Gol-dang," he said, "don't never scream like thet ag'in fer no reason. Let the thang at least git a taste of you 'fer you starts hollerin' like you's bein' et. Now tarn loose maw ha'r and neck and git down offen maw shoulders!"

Over the years, my wife has become quite an expert on reading sign, ferreting out clues here and there and matching up odd bits of trivial information from which to deduce an ingenious conclusion that couldn't make the slightest difference to anyone. I like to call her the Sherlock Holmes of sign. Just recently she came in and reported that the reason the grass in an orchard up on the hill was matted down was that a herd of elk had been sleeping there.

"Ha!" I said. "Probably just cows. What makes you think it's elk?"

"Alimentary, my dear Watson," she said. "Alimentary."

There are, of course, worse things than a smart-aleck woman. A fellow even told me what they were once, but I can never remember.

Campgrounds are my wife's favorite places for sleuthing. As soon as we arrive at a campsite, she's out of the car in a flash, reading the sign. "Party of four camped here last. Spent at least three days, I'd say from the amount of ash in the fireplace. At least one of them was a slob."

"How do you know that?"

"Threw the pull-tabs from his beer cans all over the place—boy, that's really disgusting. You'd think he'd care what kind of example he was setting for his kids."

"His kids?"

"Yeah, there are three wiener sticks leaning against the tree over there. You can see the remains of toasted-coconut-covered marshmallows on two of the sticks. Only kids can eat burnt toasted-coconut-covered marshmallows and live. Boy, if I were married to that lazy slob!" she said, holding up the third wiener stick. "Look, the wife's stick has a fork on the end of it. That's so she could cook a wiener for the old man while she was doing her own! Well, I never!"

"The guy sounds like a real slob, no doubt about it," I said. "Hey, don't throw that forked wiener stick away. You never know when something like that might come in handy."

One good thing about forked wiener sticks: It's difficult to run a person through with them.

I myself don't have much opportunity to read sign

anymore. To tell the truth, my reading tastes have changed a good deal over the years and I'd just as soon curl up with a good book or magazine. Also, books and magazines are nicer to keep around the house and you're much less likely to get dirty looks if you read them in public waiting rooms.

Tying
My Own

☞ ☞ ☞**S**omeday there will be a how-to-tie-flies book written for people like me. It will read something like this: "While holding the tying thread between two thumbs of your left hand, take a hackle feather between the big and little thumbs of your right hand . . ."

I am a person who is just naturally thumby. My eyesight isn't all that good either. When I read in a fly-tying book that I should "wrap each successive turn of tinsel next to the preceding one, edge to edge without overlapping," I can only shriek with delight and hope the author can sustain this level of humor through the rest of the book. I am seldom disappointed. Here's a line that really split my sides: "Wind the two hairs around the hook, keeping the darker one to the left." *Keeping the darker one to the left!* Oh what I wouldn't give to be able to come up with gems like that!

Contrary to the rumor spread by some of my alleged friends, I started fishing with artificial flies several years *after* the invention of the real ones, not *before.* Back when I was a kid, you could buy a good fly for fifteen cents.

And I mean a *good* fly. One Black Gnat would last you a whole season, providing you were willing to retrieve it from such receptacles as stumps submerged in rapids, thorn bushes on the sides of cliffs, and rotting logs balanced over the edges of precipices. I was always willing to retrieve it. After all, fifteen-cent flies didn't grow on trees (although a casual observer of my casting technique might assume they did). Sure, by the end of the season there would be some signs of wear and tear: the body would be on the verge of coming apart; the head, lumpy and gouged; and the general appearance, one of having been mauled and chewed on. The fly, on the other hand, would still look pretty good.

My friends and I kept count of the fish taken on each fly. Truly great flies were given names like Killer or Ol' Griz, unless, of course, they failed to attract fish on a given day, at which time they might be called simply Harold or Walter. It was not unusual for us to become quite attached to a fly. Equally common was for a fly to become attached to us. Since none of us enjoyed the prospect of having a fly surgically removed from whatever part of our anatomy it had become attached, we would occasionally pretend we were starting a new fad: wearing a fly on an ear, a shoulder blade, or an elbow. Lest the reader think we were sissies, let me hasten to add that the "surgeon" who excised the wayward fly was more often than not a burly miner (thus the expression "miner surgery"), who would haul out his pocketknife, run the flame of a kitchen match up and down the big blade a few times, order the women and children from the arena, and then say something like, "All right, you men grab hold of him and I'll have that fly out of his hide in a jiffy!"

When you found yourself in this predicament, the better part of valor if not of wisdom was simply to grab the embedded fly and remove it with a quick jerk and a muffled cry of pain, the latter sometimes causing all the cows in the vicinity to "go dry" for a month. This tactic not only saved you from "miner" surgery but for a brief period also enabled you to bait fish and fly fish simultaneously with a single hook.

The fifteen-centers were the expensive flies. The cheap flies cost about thirty-five cents a dozen and came in a little cellophane packet labeled "World's Greatest Fishing Bargain" or something like that. Neither fish nor entomologists have ever seen an insect bearing the slightest resemblance to any members of the world's greatest fishing bargain. Nevertheless, these eccentric flies served an important function: They filled up the empty space in our fly books. This function was important because the first thing you did when you and your fishing companions arrived at a fishing spot was to scoop a dead insect from the surface of the water—any bug would do—and studiously compare it with the contents of your fly book. After a couple minutes of such careful scrutiny, you would say, "By golly, I think what we have here is a hatch of black gnats." You would then take out your venerable fifteen-cent Black Gnat and tie it on. All the other guys would usually go along with this assessment unless, of course, the fifteen-center belonging to one of them happened to be a Silver Doctor or a Royal Coachman, in which case this individual would take exception to the verdict and argue heatedly that the hatch consisted of silver doctors or royal coachmen.

I must confess that if there were still good fifteen-cent flies on the market I'd hop naked on a pogo stick through a feminist picnic before I'd tie my own. But flies have gone up in price. Last summer I heard about a new pattern that was supposed to be good. My plan was to buy one, dissect it, and from the anatomical knowledge thus obtained, counterfeit a few copies. When the clerk told me the price of the fly, I was not only shocked but embarrassed. Unable to bring myself to ask if I could purchase the fly on an installment plan, I said, "Maybe I should have a look at some of your other flies."

"Oh, you mean the expensive ones," he said. "I'm sorry, but our new order hasn't come in yet."

As near as I could make out, either Lloyd's of London had refused to insure the shipment or the armored car service was late in making the delivery. It was all I could do to keep from sticking my hand in my jacket pocket, thrusting it toward the clerk, and saying, "This is a stickup! Give me all your dries, nymphs, and streamers, nothing larger than a six. And no funny stuff—this finger is loaded!"

A number of years ago—about the time investors started buying up fishing flies as a hedge against inflation —I decided that once and for all I'd better learn how to tie my own. After all, I'd been giving out advice on fly-tying for years, so I reasoned that it shouldn't be that difficult to learn how to construct the little buggers. Since I was a fly fisher of consummate skill, word spread that I knew absolutely everything there was to know about flies, including how to tie them. It beats me how a rumor like that got started, but no matter. Pretty soon, fishermen from all over came seeking my advice, and, not wishing to appear rude and secretive, I dispensed it to them freely. Although innocent of such fundamentals as how one got all those feathers and stuff to stay on a hook, I felt competent to offer consultation on the finer aspects of the art.

"I want to make some of my nymphs sink faster," a fellow said to me once. "Got any suggestions?"

"That's simple," I replied. "All you have to do is make them heavier."

"Gee, I wonder why I never thought of that," he said, and walked away shaking his head, no doubt at his own stupidity.

When the time came for me to learn how to tie my own flies, I couldn't very well ask the same people I'd been advising what tools and materials I would need to get started. If nothing else, I might have shaken their confidence in all the tips I had given them over the years. I decided the best approach would be to seek out an establishment specializing in fly-tying paraphernalia and located in an area of town where I was not likely to be recognized. I soon found just such a shop, the proprietor of which turned out to be an attractive lady of approximately my own youthful age.

"Say, don't I know you from somewhere?" she asked, scarcely before the bells on the shop's front door had ceased jangling the news of my arrival.

I smiled modestly. "Possibly you're confusing me with the actor Robert Redford, for whom I'm often mistaken despite his being of somewhat slighter build and a smidgen younger."

"No, no," she said, studying me curiously. "Now I've got it! There used to be this fellow who went fishing with my husband—Farley Quartze? I think his name was Pat or Mac or something like that, a roly-poly guy with thinning gray hair."

I was instantly overcome by pity for the frumpy wretch. Not only was the poor soul suffering from seriously impaired eyesight, she was married to a notoriously loud-mouthed know-it-all whose presence I had in fact endured on a fishing trip or two. Unless, of course, there were two Farley Quartzes, which seemed unlikely. In any case, it would not do for word to get back to *the* Farley Quartze that I had shown up at his wife's shop to buy a beginner's fly-tying outfit. There was nothing to do but pull the dubbing over the lady's lovely but afflicted eyes.

"Well, so much for chit-chat," I said, kindly. "Here's what I need. My fly-tying outfit has become such a mess, after twenty years or so of turning out thousands and thousands of flies, that I've decided to replace the whole shebang with a totally new outfit, something of professional caliber, of course. Why don't you just go ahead and whip me up one, all the usual feathers and stuff, you know?"

"Wow!" she said, staring at me in a way that I could only attribute to a momentary return of visual acuity. "That's really something! First, let me show you a really nifty little vise."

"Perhaps some other time," I replied. "Right now I think we should confine ourselves to matters related to fly-tying." The poor dear was struck speechless with disappointment by my rejection of her overture, and I couldn't help but feel sorry for her, particularly considering that she was married to an insensitive lout like Farley Quartze. Noting that she had absentmindedly extracted from a display case a tool I instantly recognized as an instrument of fly-tying, I tried to change the subject by calling her attention to it. "I see you have a hook-clamper there in your hand. I'm going to need one of those for sure, and that certainly looks like a good one."

After a moment she asked, "How long have you been tying flies?"

"You wouldn't believe me if I told you."

"Probably not," she said, and immediately began removing materials from boxes, bins, jars, and cases and stuffing them into clear plastic bags for me. I was happy to note that she was attaching to each bag a label that

identified the contents, few of which I could otherwise
have told from the plumage of a yellow-crested cuckold,
ornithology not being one of my strong points. Having
depleted the inventory of the store to her apparent
satisfaction, Mrs. Quartze began computing my bill on an
electronic calculator, her fingers dancing happily over its
buttons. For some reason, this simple exercise in digital
dexterity seemed to improve her mood just short of total
delight, and I thought the moment an appropriate one to
impress upon her that I was not only an experienced,
nay, an expert, tier of flies but also one possessed of
certain ethical standards.

"By the way," I said, surveying the mountain of
packages stuffed with furs and feathers. "I hope none of
these materials are derived from threatened or endan-
gered species."

"Like what?" she said.

"Well," I said, picking up a package and reading the
label, "like these chenilles."

Not only was Mrs. Quartze afflicted with poor vision,
but she also had the rather distasteful mannerism of
allowing her mouth to gape open every time a question
was addressed to her. "Why, no," she said presently,
regaining control of her jaw muscles, "there are plenty of
chenilles left. They reproduce faster than lemmings."

"Good to hear it," I replied. "They're such colorful
little beggars, it would be a shame if they became a
threatened species."

"Yes," she said smiling. "You'll probably be happy to
learn that the flosses are doing fine too. And the
tinsels . . ."

Well, that conversation took place many years ago. I
have since learned a good deal about the fundamentals
of fly-tying, not that I ever really believed there were

such creatures as chenilles and flosses and tinsels. That was just a little joke for the benefit of Mrs. Quartze. I don't think she got it, though, because a few days after our transaction somebody sent me a book in the mail —*Fly-tying Made Easy Even for Imbeciles*. Talk about your nerve! On the other hand, it turned out to be a pretty good book, once I got past the hard parts.

Psychic Powers
for Outdoorsmen

☞ ☞ ☞**E**ven as a child I possessed psychic powers. For example, I once was fighting with my sister, the Troll, and, as she sat on my chest braiding my fingers into a potholder, I suddenly had this vision of a snake slithering happily about in the dresser drawer where the Troll stored her fresh underwear. Naturally, I immediately dismissed the vision as preposterous. How could a simpleminded snake manage to climb the sheer side of the dresser, open a drawer, crawl inside, and finally pull the drawer shut behind? Why would a snake even want to do this? What could its motive be? The very next day, however, the Troll announced the discovery of a snake in her underwear drawer. Her announcement was made simultaneously with the discovery and had a certain operatic quality to it, beginning with a rather elaborate inhalation, which was followed by a series of staccato sounds similar to aborted sneezes, then culminated in a long, quavering, sirenlike screech, the whole perform- ance lasting not more than twenty seconds and conclud- ing with several loud thumps, these last caused by the

Troll's rebounding off the wall in an effort to get a clear shot at the bedroom door. As pure entertainment it left something to be desired, but I found the routine not to be without a certain psychological interest. As with most psychic phenomena, the mystery of the snake in the drawer and my precognition of its being there never yielded to logical inquiry, although for years afterwards the Troll insisted upon advancing a pet theory of her own as to the unknown cause of the event. No one, of course, pays much attention to the theories of a person who goes through life forking her underwear out of a drawer with a long stick.

Quite often in those days our house would be invaded by strange odors. "Smells like something died," my grandmother would say, giving me a look heavy with accusation. I would then perform an age-old rite of exorcism, which consisted of removing from a secret storage place and burying outside by the light of the moon a bait can of deteriorating worms, a collection of more-or-less drying sunfish, or possibly a box of ripening freshwater mussels. Shortly after I had performed the rite, the mysterious odor would begin to diminish in power and soon be gone altogether. My family should have been grateful that they had me around to exorcise odors, but they were generally unappreciative.

I have managed to achieve true levitation only twice. In the first instance, I not only raised the person several feet off the ground in a prone position but propelled him over a fence, across the countryside, and into his own house, where his abrupt entrance through a locked screen door caused his mother to spill a cup of hot cocoa on the cat and his father to blurt out a word that nobody supposed he even knew—or so the subject of my feat of levitation reported to me upon returning to his senses several days later.

What happened was this: A kid by the name of Lester was spending the night with me, and we were sleeping on an old mattress out in my backyard. I had complained of an earache the previous night, and my grandmother suggested that I wear something around my head to keep the cold night air from my ear. Although I possessed half a dozen stocking caps, a search of the premises unearthed not a single one of them. Finally, my grandmother said she would find me something of hers to wear. She went to a trunk in the attic and fished out one of her old bonnets, a thing made out of bearskin and which she claimed once to have worn on hayrides. At some point prior to the bonnet's being stored in the trunk for reasons of sentiment, a dog had apparently attacked it, either out of anger or fright, and had managed to tear loose several large hanks of hair, leaving in their place grotesque patches of naked skin. It fastened under the chin with two cords. Naturally, I didn't want Lester to see me wearing such a monstrosity, since he might spread rumors about me around the schoolyard, a place where rumors about me were already rampant.

I concealed the hairy bonnet inside my shirt until Lester had dozed off, rather fitfully it seemed to me, even though I had entertained him for several hours with true accounts of the numerous grisly murders that had taken place in our neighborhood and which remained unsolved. I then whipped out the bonnet, put it on, knotted the cords under my chin, and slid down under the blankets, being careful not to disturb Lester and hoping that I would be the first to awaken in the morning in order to remove the headpiece before my bedmate saw it.

Sometime during the night, as luck would have it, the bearskin bonnet became twisted around my head in such a manner that it was leaking cold air to my faulty ear and shutting it off altogether from my nose and mouth. I awoke in a panic of suffocation and tore at the knots under my chin, but to no avail. There was only one thing to do. I lunged for Lester, hoping the moon was bright enough that he could see to untie the knots. *"MOW WAAAA OOOD AAAAAAHHH!"* I shouted at him. Through a ripped seam in the bearskin, I glimpsed one of Lester's eyelids lift tentatively. Then both eyes popped open. Without further ado, Lester levitated.

After Lester's departure, I groped my way into the house to my mother's bedroom and shook Mom awake to have her untie the cords of the hairy bonnet. That's when the second levitation occurred. It was less spectacular than Lester's but every bit as good as what one might see performed on stage by the average professional magician, although, on the whole, considerably less dignified.

I also possess considerable talent for rainmaking, although only in collaboration with my friend Vern Schulze. When we were still kids, Vern and I discovered that we could produce rain any time we wished simply by going on a camping trip together. Our sleeping out in the backyard would produce a steady drizzle for most of the night. A camping trip away from home for a couple of days would call forth a series of cloudbursts that would awaken new interest in arks and set people to arguing about the meaning of "cubits." Once when we were about sixteen, we even managed to work up a major blizzard in the middle of June by going camping in the mountains for a week. We learned from that experience that the severity of the weather is in direct but inverse proportion to the warmth of the clothes we wear camping. Our light attire, appropriate to the normal weather of late June, had in that instance brought on a blizzard. If we had gone naked, we probably would have launched a new ice age.

This past summer we had not a drop of rain for nearly two months in the region where I live, and forest fires were erupting all over the place. I called up Vern.

"Vern," I said, "this drought has gone on too long. The whole country may burn up if we don't do something about it. Get your gear ready. Any questions?"

"Yeah," he replied. "Who is this?"

"You know who it is! Don't try to pull that wrong-number routine on me, Vern!"

"You must have the wrong number," he said. "There's no Vern here."

"I told you not to try that routine on me," I snapped. "Do you want to be responsible for letting the whole country go up in flames?"

"I suppose not. What's your plan?"

"Well, I figure a week-long backpacking trip into the Hoodoo Mountains would do the job."

Vern gasped. "Are you crazy? Think of the floods, man! No, three days would be more than enough! A few roads may wash out, but a three-day backpacking trip shouldn't cause any more damage than that. And it will certainly produce enough rain to put out all the forest fires."

As soon as the word got out that Vern and I were going backpacking, the local television weatherpersons began qualifying their announcements: "The official forecast is for continued hot, dry weather; however, Pat McManus and Vern Schulze are going backpacking for three days, and rains ranging from severe to torrential should be expected." Farmers, whose crops had been dying on the vine, hoisted their children to their shoulders to catch a glimpse of Vern and me as we drove by on our way to the mountains. Their wives, cheeks wet with tears of joy, waved handkerchiefs in the still air and blew us kisses. Upon being notified that our backpacking trip was under way, forest service officials began pulling in their firefighting crews. Long lines of weary, smoke-blackened firefighters cheered our two-man relief team as we passed, and fire-retardant bombers flew low over us and dipped their wings in salute. We drove on, our jaws set in grim determination.

"I sure wish they'd discover a less extreme way of making rain," Vern said. "I'm getting too old for this sort of thing."

"Me too," I said. "It wouldn't be quite so bad if they paid us to go backpacking, but when we do it for nothing, that's a lot to ask."

"Yeah," Vern said. "Say, the bridge over that dry streambed we just crossed looked a little low to me. On the way back, watch out that it's not washed away."

"Right," I said.

By the time we had hiked the first mile up the trail, we could already hear the thunder.

Materialization is one of the more difficult of the psychic arts. To perform this, I need to hike fifteen miles up a canyon to fish a stretch of water generally supposed to be barren of fish and which hasn't been visited by *Homo sapiens* since the beginning of the last century. I'll climb over giant logs, battle brush, slog through swamp, and tunnel through clouds of mosquitoes and gnats. At last I'll arrive at a long, beautiful pool at the base of a waterfall, tie on a fly, and cast out into the pool. Crazed cutthroat slightly larger than French bread boxes will rush for the fly. I'll try to set the hook too soon, and my line will whip back over my head and become one with a fifteen-foot-high bush embellished with thorns the size of ice picks. The fly will dangle down in front of my face. At that instant, three other anglers will materialize out of thin air, gather around my dangling fly, and say, "Too bad, fella. Look Fred, what he got that strike on is one of them with hackle from unhatched pterodactyl, wings of gossamer, and body wrapping from the hair of the tooth fairy. Lucky we happen to have plenty of them along."

I'm also good at dematerialization. Once, using only a map and a compass for props, I made myself and two companions vanish for three days in a Montana wilderness area. I have attempted to repeat this feat several times since and have succeeded.

Generally, however, I like to practice my dematerialization in a really wild place—Kelly's Bar & Grill. I simply say aloud the magic words, "Speaking of big fish, that reminds me of the time . . ." At that point, half of Kelly's customers will disappear with a suddenness that leaves half-filled schooners of beer suspended in mid-air.

I'm not bad at hypnosis, either. All I need to do is finish expounding on my recollection and the rest of Kelly's customers will fall into a trance or, as Kelly puts it, "stupor." (Well, one man's trance is another man's stupor.)

Even Kelly, ignorant of the psychic arts as he is, can't help but admire my powers. Quite often he will point me out to a new customer and warn, "Stay away from that guy. He's a great psycho!"

"*Psychic!*" I correct him. "A *psychic!*"

Kelly will just chortle. If there's one thing I hate more about Kelly than his abuse of words, it's his asinine chortling.

The Fishing Lesson

☞ ☞ ☞**O**ver the years, I've introduced several dozen people to the pleasures of outdoor sports. So what that some of them didn't want to be introduced! They might otherwise have ended up as criminals or drug addicts or golfers. I like to think I've had some small part in saving them from such dismal fates.

My neighbor Al Finley, the city councilperson, is a good example of what can be accomplished if you put your mind to it. Up until a few years ago, Finley had never been fishing in his life. One day he happened to mention that fact to me, and I couldn't help but feel sorry for him.

"Al," I said to him, "nobody's perfect. All of us have our faults. Want to talk about it?"

"Talk about what?" he said.

"Your degeneracy," I said.

Then he called me one of those nasty anatomical names so popular with guys who like to pretend they're tough.

174

"Listen, you dirty no-good elbow," he said, "just because I don't fish doesn't mean I'm a degenerate!"

"Somebody call me?" said Retch Sweeney, who had just walked in.

I explained to Retch that Finley had never been fishing. Retch, as a way of expressing amazement, has the irritating quirk of repeating the same rhetorical question over and over.

"You never been fishing, Al?" he asked.

"No," Finley said, irritably.

"I'll be darned, you never been fishing, hunh?"

"No!"

"That's really something! You never been fishing?"

Finley's eyes looked as if they were going to pop out of his head.

"NO!NO!NO!NO!NO!" he screamed. "I HAVE NEVER BEEN FISHING, NOT ONCE IN MY WHOLE BLINKETY-BLANK LIFE, YOU FRACTURED KNEE-CAP!"

"Well, that's probably what makes you so irritable," Retch said.

After I had helped pry Finley's thumbs off of Retch's windpipe and they had both calmed down, I suggested that the three of us take a little fishing trip together. Neither one of them was too happy with the idea at first, but I eventually brought them around.

"Hell, Finley," I said, "take a few days off from City Hall. The taxpayers can use the rest. Besides, learning to fish will open up a whole new way of life to you."

Once he sets his mind to do something, Finley goes all the way. He rushed out and bought himself rods, reels, lines, leaders, hooks, creel, waders, fishing vest, etc. He practically cleaned out the local sporting-goods stores. What made me mad wasn't that he put together a better fishing outfit than mine but that the city's rate for garbage collection went up in direct proportion to what he spent. If I had suggested an African safari to him, we wouldn't have been able to afford garbage anymore.

The night before we were to leave on the fishing trip, Retch and I went over to Finley's place to make sure he was properly outfitted and to make last-minute arrangements. Finley was flitting about getting his stuff ready, and it was enough to make a petrified toad smile.

He had everything arranged in neat little piles according to function, size, color, etc. His tackle box alone was so neat and orderly it was pathetic.

Retch looked at it and grinned. "This will never do, Finley."

"Why not?" Finley growled.

"It just don't look right," Retch said. "It ain't got any character. What you need is a good snarl of leader in there with sinkers and hooks and maybe a dried worm still attached. And it ain't very efficient either. With my lures, I just keep them all dumped together down in the bottom of the box. Then all I got to do is grab one of them and they all come out in a big clump. I just turn the big clump around till I find something that looks good and pluck it off. You gonna waste a lotta time pokin' around through all them compartments."

Finley was obviously embarrassed by his own ineptness in organizing a tackle box. Still, that was no reason for him to refer to Retch as an "ingrown toenail." Retch may not be smart, but he has feelings just like anyone else.

Retch and I did everything we could to help Finley get his stuff into some kind of respectable condition so we all wouldn't be embarrassed if we ran into other anglers on the river. But Finley said he liked for his stuff to look neat and clean and brand new. He wouldn't even let me smear some salmon-egg clusters on his fishing vest or leak some dry-fly dressing on his shirt.

Finally, Retch could stand it no longer. He grabbed Finley's hat, threw it on the floor, and jumped up and down on it.

"Now, that looks more like a fishing hat," he said, holding it up for approval.

"I can see that, you shinbone," Finley said. "Too bad it isn't my *fishing* hat!" Turned out it was his politicking hat.

Retch and I had a good chuckle over the little misunderstanding, and even Finley was mildly amused by it, although not until several years later.

To make amends, Retch offered to let Finley stomp on *his* fishing hat. Finley said all right but only if Retch would agree to leave his head in it.

I could see that Finley was becoming irritated, since he had acquired a rather severe twitch in his left eye and was pacing back and forth popping his knuckles. It was apparent that all those years without fishing had taken their toll on his nervous system. I tried to be as gentle as I could in giving him the last few bits of essential information about our fishing trip.

"I've got some bad news and some good news for you, Al," I said.

"What? Tell me. I can hardly wait."

"First, the bad news. The road into the Big Muddy, which is where we're going to fish, is pretty treacherous—steep, winding, narrow, washouts, logging trucks, that sort of thing."

"The good news?"

"We're taking your car, and you get to drive."

"What's so good about that?"

"Well, there are several high old wood bridges where Retch and I have to get out and walk across just to make sure they're safe for you to drive over. Then there's the stretch of road along the top of Bottomless Canyon, where we have to get out again and guide you along just to make sure your outside tires don't hang so far out in space they might slip off. Hell, all that walking would sap your energy, and we want you to save it for fishing."

"I see, I see," Finley said, twitching and popping.

The plan we worked out was for Finley to pick us up at three in the morning. Finley, not knowing anything about fishing, expressed some amazement at the early hour for getting started. We explained that it was necessary if we were to catch the first feed on the Big Muddy.

"And don't be late," Retch said. "The one sin I can't forgive is for a guy to be late for a fishing trip."

The resulting foul-up was probably my fault. I should have taken into account the fact that Finley knew absolutely nothing about fishing and its practitioners, and I should have explained the nuances more thoroughly to him. Right in the middle of the night, I was awakened from a deep sleep by a horn blaring in my driveway. I got up and staggered over to a window to look out.

"What is it?" my wife mumbled.

"I don't know," I said. "Some maniac is down in our driveway honking his fool horn off. What kind of a person honks his horn in front of your house at three A.M.?"

It was Finley, of course. As I stuffed my gear into the back of his station wagon, I tried to be as kind as possible.

"Al," I said, "when a fisherman says he is leaving on a fishing trip at exactly, absolutely and positively, three A.M., he means five-thirty at the earliest. If he's leaving at three, he says midnight."

After we had honked Retch out of bed, he staggered to the car looking like something put together by an inept taxidermist.

"Wha-what is it?" he said. "The dam bust? We gonna be flooded?"

By four we were on the road, pumping hot coffee into our veins from the thermos Finley had had the good sense to bring along. In a little while, we felt good. There is nothing better than to be headed into the mountains on a clean fresh day with the sun rising through the trees and good company and good talk and the sense of ease that comes from the knowledge that you are in somebody else's car and it is not your transmission that is going to get torn out on a big rock. Even Finley seemed to be enjoying himself. Then we came to the road that leads up to the headwaters of the Big Muddy.

"Hang a left there," I told Finley.

"A left where? All I see is that rock slide coming down off the mountain."

"That's it, buddy," I said. "By the way, Al, how do you feel about transmissions? You don't strike me as the sort of man who would develop an attachment to them."

I am happy to report that Finley is a superb driver and negotiated the Big Muddy road without the slightest damage to his car. In fact, the only incident worth reporting was when the car started to teeter on the edge of a washout and Finley became confused and jumped out of the car at the same time Retch and I did. When we explained to him that we had merely had a sudden urge to check the huckleberry crop along the road, he climbed back in and drove around the washout, by which time Retch and I had pretty well exhausted our interest in the huckleberry crop and were able to rejoin him.

"Why is it that every time we come to a bad stretch of

road, you two are overpowered by an urge to leap out and study the local flora?" Finley asked, mopping the sweat off his brow so it wouldn't drip into his twitching eye.

"Must be just a coincidence," I said. "Say, isn't that a beautiful specimen of Birdwell's lichen on those rocks up ahead there?"

"You mean up there where the road seems to be cracking off from the side of the cliff?"

"That's it, buddy," I said, opening the door. "Remind me sometime to show you my extensive collection of lichen."

As I say, we arrived at the Big Muddy without incident, and aside from the fact that Finley went about for some time afterwards with his hands shaped as though they were still gripping a steering wheel, we were all in fine fettle and high spirits. Finley even commented that he didn't know how he had managed to get through forty-three years of life without fishing, he was having so much fun.

"You ain't seen nothing yet," Retch told him. "Just wait till you actually start fishing."

"I can hardly contain myself," Finley said.

Retch and I helped Finley rig up his tackle, and then we all cut down through the brush toward the Big Muddy. It was rough going, and the mosquitoes came at us like mess call at a fat farm. I led the way and did the best I could to point out the obstacles to the other two, but apparently I stepped right over one beaver hole without noticing it. Suddenly I heard a strange sound and turned around to see what it was. I was shocked. There was Finley's head resting on the ground, its eyes still blinking in disbelief! It was about as horrible a thing as I've ever seen. Then the head spoke to me.

"You *gluteus maximus*," it said. "Why didn't you tell me about this hole?"

"I didn't see it, head," I replied. "It looks pretty deep though—we better warn Retch about it."

"Ha!" Finley said. "Whose shoulders do you think I'm standing on?"

That was about the only real catastrophe to befall us. The rest of the day was pretty much your routine fishing trip. Oh, Finley did lose his sack lunch and made quite a fuss about that, but it was nothing really. As far as we could figure out, the lunch apparently washed out of the pocket in the back of his fishing vest. There was a pretty strong current at the place where he was trying to swim to the north bank of the Big Muddy, and that was probably when his lunch washed away. Actually, I had thought there were good odds that Finley would make it all the way across that high log over the river, even if he was running. But before Retch and I could shake hands on our bet, he ran right off into space and dropped like a shot into the river. Of course, I hadn't taken into account the fact that he was holding up his pants with one hand and had all those yellow jackets swarming around him. I had told Finley that yellow jackets sometimes hole up in old brush piles and don't like to be disturbed, but he didn't listen. I won't go into how he was disturbing them or why he was holding up his pants with one hand, because it isn't especially interesting. Anyway, to hear Finley tell it, you would think he was the only fisherman to have such an experience. You would think Retch and I had personally put those yellow jackets under that brush pile.

"Look, Finley," I told him, "it's no big deal. Fishermen lose their lunches all the time."

I dug a sandwich out of my own fishing vest and gave

it to him and patted him on the shoulder. He stared down at the sandwich. "Looks like peanut butter and jelly," he said.

I didn't have the heart to tell him it was supposed to be just peanut butter, even though I could have put those salmon eggs to good use. He didn't seem to notice, anyway.

One of the most difficult things about introducing a guy to the sport of fishing is determining whether it has taken hold on him. Finley had done so much complaining all day, I couldn't be sure. As we were driving back into town, I decided to ask him.

"I'm of two minds about it," he replied. "One bad and one good."

"What's the bad?"

"I won't be able to get out of bed for a week."

"What's the good?"

"Next time we're taking *his* car."

"Whose car?" Retch said.

"Yours, armpit, that's whose," he said.

I could see Finley was hooked. Already he had picked up one of the most important techniques.

The Hunting Camp

☞ ☞ ☞ The guys and I were practicing our lies down at Kelly's Bar & Grill the other night, and before I knew it Fred Smits had got started on a long and boring tale about one of his hunting trips. Something of an expert on long and boring tales, I can usually spot one and snuff it out while it is still in the larval stage. On this occasion, however, Mavis, Kelly's barmaid, had just leaned over my shoulder to replenish the beverages at our table. At that instant I noticed something flutter into my drink. At first glance it appeared to be an emaciated centipede. Since Kelly's is not exactly a showcase of the County Health Department, it was only natural for me to assume that the creature had lost its grip while being pursued across the ceiling by a pack of cockroaches. I shrank back in disgust from the loathsome creature and began to stab at it with a pepperoni stick in the hope of either flipping it out of my glass or drowning it before it drank too much.

Without warning, Mavis grabbed the pepperoni stick

and, trying to wrench it away from me, hissed in my ear, "It's mine, you idiot! Give it back!"

Mavis not seeming the type to own a starving centipede, I quite logically leaped to the conclusion that she was referring to my pepperoni stick. "It is not yours," I snapped. "It's mine, I bought it, and I'm going to eat the darn thing!"

This simple assertion seemed to touch off a burst of maniacal strength in Mavis, and, gasping with rage, she twisted my wrist back in such a manner that she was able to remove from the tip of the pepperoni stick the sodden centipede. She then stalked off, sniffling something about my trying to eat her eyelash!

Her eyelash, for pity's sake! It should be easy for anyone to understand how a man of my sensitivity would be upset by such a bizarre assault on his person and character, not to mention his pepperoni. I relate this dreadful experience only by way of indicating the magnitude of event necessary to distract me sufficiently that someone is allowed to get a long and boring tale under way without having it instantly snuffed. By the time I tuned in, Fred had covered the first couple hours preceding the hunt, leaving no detail unturned, no matter how lacking in relevance or consequence. The other guys at the table had already been poleaxed by trivia and were staring catatonically at Fred as he droned on: "So a couple of minutes after Ralph knocked the ash off his cigar, we pulled off the road and made camp, and then me and Ralph starts up the trail to look for deer sign and I steps on a twig but it don't make no noise 'cause it's wet—did I say it rained the night before? Anyway . . ."

"Hold it right there, Fred," I said, noticing how barren of detail was the reference to making camp. "Did you say 'made camp'?"

"Yeh. Now where was I? Did I tell you the part about the wet twig?"

"C'mon, Fred, don't try to weasel out of it," I said. "Admit that all you did was turn off the ignition on your camper truck and set the hand brake. That doesn't constitute making camp."

"We had to let down the camper jacks, too," he said sheepishly, looking about the circle of faces, which had suddenly filled with accusation.

I shook my head. "You know the rules, Fred. It's all right to lie about unimportant things as long as it's entertaining. Add a few points to your buck, a few inches to your trout, a few miles to a trail—but don't ever say you *made camp* when you didn't."

"I'm sorry, I'm sorry!" he cried. "I don't know what came over me. It just slipped out."

"All right," I said, patting his hand. "We'll forgive you this time. Just don't ever let it happen again." Snuffing out a long and boring tale can sometimes be cruel, but it has to be done.

Then Fred made his second blunder of the evening. He looked at me and, in a penitent tone, asked, "Say, Pat, just what does constitute making camp on a hunting trip?"

Well, if that didn't create an uproar! Everyone started jumping up and down and shouting threats at Fred, and the situation looked as if it might turn ugly. Then Kelly got out his baseball bat from behind the bar and charged over. By the time the fellows had got him calmed down and made him promise not to try to hit Fred with the bat, I had managed to scribble out an outline and a few rough notes on a napkin.

"I'm glad you asked that question," I said. "I can certainly tell you what constitutes making a hunting camp, but it may take a while, so you fellows might just as well sit down and relax."

They sank into their chairs, muttering.

"I'll have to ask you mutterers to be quiet," I said.

"Watch da language," Kelly said. "Dis is a nice bar."

Since he was still fingering the bat in a psychotic manner, I resisted the impulse to retort and got my lecture started. It went something like this.

The first hunting camps were invented by prehistoric man, who divided his time equally between hunting for wild meat and having wild meat hunt for him. Interestingly, if a man made a hunting camp when he should have made a hunted camp, he was thereafter referred to as "et." (As in: "How come I never see Iggy around anymore?" "Got et.")

The hunting camp consisted of nothing more than a few branches thrown on the ground for a bed, whereas the hunted camp utilized but a single branch, one attached to the upper part of a tall tree, where the hunted would spend the night standing on it. Occasionally, a fun-loving catamount would climb the tree and send the men fleeing wildly among the branches. From this activity arose the expression "tearing limb from limb." Usually, however, the hunted camp provided adequate security, not to mention a cure for sleepwalking.

These prehistoric hunters were the first to come up with that boon to camping, the shelter. The first shelters, simple affairs made of rock, eventually came to be called caves, after the cavemen who lived in them. Unlike the hunted camp, the caves provided protection from wind and rain as well as from wild beasts, but they made for a heavy pack on a long trip.

Since matches and camp stoves had not yet been invented, primitive man was forced to carry his campfire right along with him from place to place. Archeologists believe this may explain why hunting camps in those days were located only ten yards apart. These early firebearers are thought to have contributed to mankind the ten-yard dash and also the expressions "Ow!" "Ouch!" "Yipe!" and *"Bleeping bleep-of-a-bleep!"*

Harsh as these early camps may have been, they probably had a great many similarities to the hunting camps of today. Indeed, it is not hard to imagine the following conversation occurring around one of their prehistoric campfires.

"All right, who forgot to bring the salt? If there's one thing I hate it's pterodactyl wing without salt!"

"Squatty was supposed to bring it."

"The heck I was. I carry the cave, remember? It's Pudd's job to bring the salt."

"Ow! Ouch! Yipe! No sir! I carried the *bleeping bleep-of-a-bleep* fire!"

There is some evidence that early man very nearly invented the interior-frame umbrella tent. Apparently, a hunter one day got the idea of stretching dried skins over a framework of poles he had lashed together. The contraption aroused a great deal of curiosity among his fellow hunters, who up to that time had thought the man an imbecile.

"What is it?" they asked him.

"A brontosaurus trap," he replied.

His fellow hunters concluded that the man was indeed an imbecile. Because of his quick-witted reply, however, the anonymous inventor saved countless generations from the agony of pitching interior-frame umbrella tents, and he thus came to be regarded as one of the great benefactors of mankind.

Before the invention of sleeping bags, the hides of hairy mammoths and saber-toothed tigers provided cozy warmth through the long nights of the approaching ice age, but, unfortunately, only for hairy mammoths and saber-toothed tigers. Early cave paintings, however, indicate that one group of prehistoric hunters devised a clever substitute for a sleeping bag. They would lure a saber-toothed tiger into their cave, where one of the hunters would knock it out with a club. Then the hunters would all lie down in a row and tug the tiger up over them for warmth and try to get a few hours of sleep before the beast regained consciousness. The little band of hunters is thought to have vanished suddenly and mysteriously. The only theory for their disappearance that archeologists can offer is that one night the man in charge of the club forgot to put the cat out.

At this point in my lecture, Kelly began to shout incoherently and had to be wrestled back into his chair and disarmed of the baseball bat.

"All right," I said. "So much for the history of hunting camps. I will now move right along to my analysis of the phenomenon known as the modern hunting camp." And I did.

First off, as I told the boys at Kelly's, I don't consider anything that's comfortable a camp. I know one guy who goes hunting in a $50,000 motor home that has everything but a front lawn and a basement. Driving a hunting camp fifty-five miles an hour down a freeway goes against everything I believe in, and I simply won't stand for it. A hunting camp, after all, is not so much a thing as a state of mind.

Mention the phrase "hunting camp" to any hunter worth his fluorescent-orange vest and the picture that immediately leaps into his mind is this: A classic cabin-style tent, suspended from a framework of slender, unpeeled saplings that have been lashed together by the hunters, is situated on a flat, stoneless, grassy piece of ground with a backdrop of evergreens, tastefully splotched here and there with patches of autumn color. The pipe of a wood-burning stove pokes up through the roof of the tent. A small, pure, ice-cold mountain stream tumbles among boulders off to one side. From a stout tree limb dangles the standard fourteen-point buck. One of the hunters is splitting the evening's firewood from blocks that are miraculously dry, straight of grain, and the right length. The other hunter is pouring himself a steaming cup of hot coffee from the pot hung over the near-smokeless campfire. There are no insects in the picture, and the only snow glistens on a distant peak, made rosy by the sun setting gloriously in the west.

This picture, of course, represents the ideal of the hunting camp, which is seldom if ever achieved. The average hunting camp, infinite in its variety, falls somewhat short of the ideal. Here are but a few versions of it:

THE NO-FRILLS CAMP—This is the camp that is resorted to upon arriving at the hunting site very late on a cold and rainy night. One of the hunters will suggest something like this: "Hell, why don't we just sleep in the car. It's only five or six hours until dawn." A curious aftermath of the no-frills camp is that the hunter who suggested it is not spoken to again by any of the other hunters for approximately six months. The no-frills camp may be injurious to your health, but only if you should greet one of the occupants of it too cheerfully on the following morning.

THE FLAT CAMP—This is the camp that is resorted to after someone asks, "Okay, where are the tent poles? Who put them in the car?" And nobody answers.

THE SLANT CAMP—The commonest of all camps used in the mountains, the slant camp is the source of several interesting phenomena, one of which is that anytime something is dropped, it falls horizontally. Several times I myself have seen men encased in sleeping bags shoot out through the side of a slant camp tent like a burial at sea. One of the drawbacks of the slant camp is that by the middle of the night all the sleeping hunters are stacked on one another at the low side of the tent. And the guy on the bottom is always the one who drank a beer before turning in.

THE HANG-GLIDER CAMP—This camp results from the suggestion, "Let's pitch the tent right on top of the peak. That way the wind will blow the insects away from us."

THE HORSE CAMP—Where everyone except the packer eats standing up.

THE DOUBLE-BARREL CAMP—Where . . .

At this point, my lecture was interrupted by Mavis, who had returned sullenly to replenish our beverages. As luck would have it, her eyelash plopped into my drink again. I fished it out with a toothpick and handed it to her. You've never heard such screaming. I told Kelly afterwards, "Either fatten up these centipedes or make Mavis get rid of the false eyelashes. Otherwise, I'm not going to give any more lectures in this establishment."

So far, he has failed to heed my warning.

If You Don't Mind, I'll Do It Myself!

☞ ☞ ☞ **A**ll together, I was off the stuff for nearly six weeks. Did it cold turkey, too. Then I couldn't stand it any longer and sneaked down to the basement for a quicky, just a little something to steady my nerves. But one of the girls caught me at it and rushed upstairs to tell her mother. I could hear her in the kitchen, sobbing out the news of my relapse.

"I just found Dad hiding in the coalbin, and he's at it again."

"Oh dear! I was afraid of this!" my wife exclaimed. "I thought I had gotten rid of them all, but he probably had one stashed away under the coal."

Another kid wandered into the kitchen. "What's all the ruckus?"

"Your father's hitting the kits again."

"Figures. What is it this time?"

"Looks like another muzzleloader," the informer said.

My wife moaned. "I tried to get him to take the cure."

"Actually, there's no cure for do-it-yourselfism," Big

Mouth said. "Our school brought in a do-it-yourself addict to tell us kids how he got hooked on the habit. He said a friend of his got him tying his own fishing flies. Then he started refinishing his own split-bamboo rods. Before he knew it, he was into the hard stuff—making his own surf-casting rods, mountain tents, muzzle-loaders . . ."

"Oh, don't I know!" my wife said.

"The really terrible thing," the kid went on, "was that while this guy was talking to us, he rewired the teacher's reading lamp, overhauled the pencil sharpener, and was starting to sand the desk tops when his attendants dragged him off."

Well, everybody's got to have a hobby of some kind, I always say. And the next time I go on the wagon, I'm going to make it myself. I've never built a wagon before.

There's a lot of prejudice against us do-it-yourselfers. Most of it derives from jealousy. Take my neighbor, Al Finley, for instance. He had to give up headaches because he couldn't figure out how to get the tops off the new child-proof aspirin bottles. But do you think he would admit his incompetence? Not a chance.

"I prefer to buy my stuff ready-made," he told me a couple years ago. "If I wanted to waste my time doing it myself, I certainly could. I'm pretty good with tools, even though I just keep the basic ones around the house—a pounder, a screwturner, and one of those cutters with the sharp little points . . ."

"A saw?"

Finley sniffed. "You do-it-yourselfers just love to toss that technical jargon up at a fellow, don't you?"

"Not especially," I replied. "But now that you mention it, I'd appreciate your returning the squeezer you borrowed from me. You're never going to get the top off that aspirin bottle anyway."

Usually, I can just shrug off the nasty cracks hurled at us do-it-yourselfers, but once in a while they get to me. When I built my kids a sleek little soap-box racer, Finley leaned over the fence and asked me why I was putting wheels on a packing crate. That was bad enough, but when I built my dog a new house, employing some of the most advanced designs and technology of modern architecture, Finley called up on the phone and hissed into my ear:

"Don't make a sound! Some kind of huge, squat, brown, ugly creature has landed in your backyard! And that's not the worst!"

"What's the worst, Finley?"

"The worst is, I just saw it eat your dog! Har, har, har!"

Three questions instantly crossed my mind: Is it possible to cement a man's mouth shut while he is sleeping? Would it be considered a crime or, in Finley's case, a public service? And finally, would he be awakened by the sound of a pre-mix truck backing up to his bedroom window?

I must admit that do-it-yourselfism may be getting a bit out of hand in this country. There are do-it-yourself baby deliveries, do-it-yourself marriages, do-it-yourself divorces, and do-it-yourself funerals. If there were a kit and a set of instructions, there are probably people who would undertake do-it-yourself brain surgery. In fact, I once gave myself a haircut that was commonly mistaken for brain surgery.

Although I will tackle just about any do-it-yourself project, my specialty is outdoor gear. Nowadays I prefer to work with store-bought kits, but back when I was a youngster and just getting started on do-it-yourselfism, there weren't any kits on the market. You had to make your own kits.

The way you made a kit was to wander around gathering up the necessary parts as you found them. You then threw the parts into a large, handy container, often referred to as your bedroom. This procedure usually presented no problem if you were putting together a simple kit, like for a slingshot. On the other hand, if you were putting together a more complex kit, like for a four-wheel-drive ATV, family relations could become strained. I recall one particularly ugly scene with my mother, grandmother, and sister. To have heard them rave and carry on you would have thought there was something abnormal about a kid's bedroom leaking crankcase oil.

I have since read in child psychology books that parents are supposed to give their children "positive reinforcement" as a means of stimulating their creative urges. My family never gave *me* any positive reinforcement. The following account is an example of their narrow-minded and negative attitudes.

The peaceful quiet of a warm fall afternoon was suddenly shattered by a shrill scream from my sister. "There's something decaying in his bedroom! I know there is!"

"Nonsense!" I exclaimed. It was a pretty good word for a ten-year-old, and I exclaimed it every chance I got.

My mother and grandmother appeared at the bottom of the stairs. They conferred a moment and then, without warning, charged. I tried to bar the door but was too late. Gram got her foot in the crack, and they started forcing their way in.

"Most likely he caged some poor animal in there and let it starve to death," Gram said, reaching around the door and trying to swat me out of the way.

I ducked. "I wouldn't do anything like that."

"How about the worms, young man?" Mom snarled. "You remember the can of worms you left under the stairs last July?"

Then they burst in upon me, their fierce feminist eyes sweeping over the various kits in progress.

"There it is," Gram shouted. "Land sakes, what did I tell you? Just look what he's done to that poor creature!"

Horrified, my mother sucked in her breath. Even I could have told her that it's unwise to suck in one's breath in close proximity to a deer hide being tanned by a ten-year-old boy in a closed bedroom during an unseasonably warm fall. Her reaction was impressive and well worth observing from a scientific viewpoint. Nevertheless, I'm almost certain that there have been longer and more sustained fits of gagging, and for her to claim a record was sheer nonsense, as was her charge that she had suffered permanent damage to her olfactory system. I proved on several later occasions that her sense of smell was fully intact.

My reason for tanning the deer hide, a donation from a hunter I knew, was to put together a kit for making myself a suit of buckskins. I had used an old Indian recipe for my tanning solution, but I should have known that the old Indian was pulling a fast one on me because of the way he kept wiping smiles off his face. Some of the ingredients seemed pretty ridiculous to me at the time, but lots of things seem ridiculous to a ten-year-old, so I couldn't go by that. Probably it would have served Pinto Jack right if I had told Mom that he was the hunter who had given me the deer hide in the first place.

"You ever get your hide tanned?" Pinto Jack asked me some time later.

"Darned near did," I said. "But it's hard for a woman

to run and gag at the same time, particularly when she's carrying a rake handle."

Over the years I put together kits for bows and arrows, dogsleds, snowshoes, packframes, tents, caves, log cabins, canoes, a forty-foot sportfisher, and dozens of other neat things I can no longer recall. The kits eventually flowed out of my bedroom, through the house, into the yard, filled up the outbuildings, and started spreading over the fields. The neighbors considered me an unnatural disaster and worried that their own lands would soon be inundated by my kits. One old neighbor lady complained to my mother that she and her husband lived with their bags packed and in fear that my kits would break loose without warning and flow over them in the middle of the night before they could flee. Another neighbor accused me of stunting his potato crop, which was absurd. A forty-foot sportfisher just doesn't shade that much ground, except possibly in the late afternoon. Nevertheless, tiring of the constant stream of complaints and periodic attempts on my life, I finally curtailed my output of kits and construction projects in general and took up with girls as a means of filling in my spare time. Girls eventually turned out to be almost as interesting as kits, and they didn't take up so much space.

Over the years, I have learned a good deal about putting together do-it-yourself kits, and I herewith pass on to the reader a few helpful hints.

Never buy a beginner's kit. It is much more interesting to jump in at an advanced stage and strike out from there. After you have mastered a particular skill, you can always go back and pick up the basics. Nothing stimulates a high level of interest like a good dose of desperation.

After you have put together a firearm of any kind,

be sure to take the following safety precautions when you test fire it. First, it is absolutely essential to carry a pair of sunglasses with you when you drive out to the firing range. Never test fire a homemade firearm when you are alone; always take a friend along. Then, load the firearm in strict accordance to the standard procedures. Finally, hand the firearm to your friend and say, "Here, why don't you fire off a few rounds? I forgot my sunglasses in the car and have to go back and get them."

Over the years, I've learned that it never pays to publicly put a name to the results of one of my do-it-yourself projects. For example, when I made myself a really superb goose-down hunting jacket, other hunters I happened to meet in the woods would ask me why I was wearing a red sleeping bag. Actually, it isn't at all difficult to come up with a good many sound reasons for wearing a red sleeping bag, particularly if you give the subject a little thought.

Another good strategy is just to make up an appropriate name. Say, you've just put together a mountain-tent kit, but it didn't turn out quite right. Now if your friends happen by and ask what it is, you're going to be subjected to a lot of ridicule, or worse yet, sympathy, if you identify the object as a mountain tent. So what you do is call it a flamph.

"A flamph?" they will say.

"Yeah, a portable flamph."

"What's it for?"

"For sleeping in up in the mountains."

"Hey, man, that's pretty neat, kind of like a mountain tent, hunh?"

The final precaution is this: Never encourage do-it-yourselfism among your immediate neighbors. I know this because Finley finally caught the do-it-yourself bug from me. One day I saw him out in the backyard working away feverishly with his pounder and cutter and my squeezer.

"What are you doing?" I asked, forgetting to restrain a contemptuous laugh.

"Building a boat," he replied matter-of-factly.

"A toy boat?"

"No, a real boat."

I must say his antics provided me with a good deal of amusement. When he finally had it finished, I couldn't resist one final little jab at him.

"Tell me this, Finley, what kind of boat is that?"

"A flumph," he said.

Well, he had me there. There's just no way you can say a flumph doesn't look like a flumph. The one thing that I can say about the damn thing is that it has stunted the growth of my potatoes. A forty-foot flumph shades a lot more ground than you might think.

Useful
Outdoor Comments

☞ ☞ ☞ **E**very year thousands of sportspersons suffer unnecessary ridicule because they don't know the proper comments to make in particular outdoor situations. Merely extracting one's self from a predicament is insufficient; one must do so with grace and style. The proper comment not only enables one to prevail over embarrassment but, in many instances, even to survive.

Consider the following case: When my nephew Shaun and his friend Eddie were about twelve, they considered themselves to be master woodsmen. They demanded to be hauled out to a remote campsite and left to survive for four days with nothing but a handful of matches, their sheath knives, sleeping bags, a small tent, and forty pounds of food. I drove them to the campsite and dropped them off, giving each a firm handshake and a manly look in the eye to let them know how much I respected their courage and that I never expected to see either of them again.

On the second day of their adventure, Shaun's

mother, my sister, had to be epeatedly and forcibly detached from the walls she insisted upon climbing. That day, too, one of the worst rainstorms in the history of our county struck and continued on through the night. The next morning my sister argued persuasively that the time had come for me to retrieve the boys, which I set about doing the very instant I pried her thumbs off my Adam's apple.

As I arrived at the campsite, an ominous feeling settled over me. The rain had scarcely subsided to a downpour, and the clouds of mist hung in the trees. There was no sign of the boys, except for the soggy remains of a campfire and the pitiful little tent. They had pitched the tent in a low area, and the waves of a shallow lake now lapped its walls. I waded into the lake, pulled back the entrance flap, and peered hesitantly inside. Shaun and Eddie, encased in their sleeping bags and awash in a foot of water, peered back. Both looked embarrassed. Several seconds passed before Shaun spoke.

"Well, so much for woodcraft," he said.

Right then I knew that Shaun was a master woodsman and that there was nothing more I could teach him—except possibly the feasibility of pitching one's tent on high ground. He had said the perfect thing for the situation and, in so doing, had triumphed over it. Even his posture and facial expression were exactly right: body prone, limp, waterlogged; eyes telling mutely about the other side of despair; pale lips moving just enough to deliver the appropriate comment in a matter-of-fact tone: "Well, so much for woodcraft." Perfect!

Since then I have found countless opportunities in which to use a paraphrase of his comment:

"Well, so much for mountain climbing."

"Well, so much for scuba diving."

'Well, so much for flying lessons."
"Well, so much for seven-X leaders."
"Well, so much for sex."
"Well, so much for shooting rapids."
"Well, so much for sex while shooting rapids."

As a service to my readers, I have put together a compendium of situations and appropriate responses. It is my hope that these recommendations will be studied carefully and will enable you to comport yourself properly in the outdoors and in a manner worthy of a sportsman.

SITUATION—You have climbed into your mummy-style sleeping bag, wiggled around to sort the rocks under your Ensolit pad according to size and shape, and finally are about to drift into peaceful sleep. Then you detect what appears at first to be a minor problem—the wool sock on your left foot has become partially pulled off.

A partially pulled-off sock does not pose a threat to one's continued existence. On the other hand, it is not the sort of thing that can be totally ignored. It gives one the feeling that all is not right with the world, that everything is not in its proper place, performing its designated function in the prescribed and traditional manner. A partially pulled-off sock is an irritation, perhaps not one of the magnitude of, say, a mosquito walking around inside one's ear or nostril, but an irritation nevertheless.

After twisting and turning in your sleeping bag for some time, telling yourself that the sock is of no consequence, you at last arrive at the conclusion that it will drive you absolutely mad if you allow it to continue its insubordination for another minute. The simplest way in which to settle the matter is to unzip your sleeping bag, sit up, and pull the sock back on with a firm and reprimanding jerk. The problem is that unzipping the bag will invite in a blast of cold air, which will then require turning your metabolism back on to get everything warmed up again, and that in turn will result in your staying awake until you are once more nice and cozy. Another problem is that your previous twisting and turning have relocated the sleeping bag zipper between your shoulder blades at the top and your *peroneus longus* at the bottom. You therefore decide to try pulling up the sock without unzipping the bag.

Your first thought is that you can simply raise your leg high enough so that you can reach the sock. But no, your leg wedges against the sides of the bag, keeping the sock just a few inches out of reach of your clawing fingers. This effort has caused you to become turned at right angles to your Ensolite pad, but no matter; the contest with the sock has now engaged your honor. Since there is more room in the top of the bag, you now reason that by tilting your head forward onto your chest, you should be able to double over enough to get a grip on the sock. As you execute this maneuver, the nylon bag squeaks from the strain and squeezes your shoulders in against your ears. You are now locked into a semi-prenatal position inside the bag, presenting a spectacle that an outside observer could not help but compare to a defective German sausage in need of recall. But at last you have the offending wool in hand and pull it back on your foot with a pained but satisfying grunt. All that remains to be done now is to extract yourself from your compressed posture. Alas, the gentle slope you selected for a bedsite begins to take an active and aggressive role in compounding your plight. You topple over onto your side. With herculean effort and gasped curses that would provoke envy in a Marine drill sergeant, you manage to roll onto your knees. This is immediately determined to be a mistake, since it leads to a series of flopping somersaults down the incline, which becomes increasingly steeper. You come to rest jammed under a fallen tree fifty feet or so away from your starting point.

In the morning your companions get up, stare with some puzzlement at your vacated Ensolite pad, shrug, and begin preparing breakfast. Eventually you are discovered under the tree and extricated. At this moment you can either suffer ridicule or you can make the appropriate comment and earn your companions' everlasting respect and esteem. ("Everlasting" nowadays means approximately two weeks.)

What, then, is the proper response in this situation? Whining and inane jabber about a partially pulled-off sock simply won't cut it, particularly if you insist upon hobbling about in the posture of a chimpanzee with lumbago. Here's what you do: Smile, yawn, stretch luxuriously, and, as soon as your vertebrae cease their popping and pinging, say with a slightly lascivious chuckle, "Boy, I didn't think they made dreams like that anymore!"

SITUATION—The bush pilot returns to pick up you and your companion after a week of fishing on a wilderness lake. "Now you fellas are about to enjoy some real sporty flying," he says. "Did you notice how on my takeoff from here last week I had to flip this old crate over on her side when I went between those two tall pine trees and then how I stood her right up on her tail to get over that ridge?" He now doubles over with laughter and pounds his knee as you and your partner exchange glances. "Well," the pilot continues, "with the two of you and your canoe and all your gear on board, the takeoff is gonna be a little tricky this time. What I was wonderin' is if maybe I could get each of you fellas to straddle a pontoon, and if we come up a little short on the ridge there, maybe you could just sort of walk us right on over the top. How does that strike you?"

Naturally, it will be difficult for you and your partner to contain your joy at the prospect of being allowed in this way to assist in the takeoff. Since it is considered bad form to jump up and down and clap your hands in glee, you must restrict yourself to a few lip tremors and an eye twitch or two.

The important thing to keep in mind in selecting just the right response in this situation is that the pilot is probably joshing you. Therefore, you just shrug and say, "Which pontoon do you want me on?" If he isn't joshing, remember to walk really fast as you go over the ridge.

SITUATION—Back when I was about fifteen, my stepfather, Hank, and I drove out to the neighboring county to fish a stream that meandered through a series of dilapidated farms, none of which showed any visible means of support. After the day's fishing, we returned to our car to find that someone had stolen our battery. My stepfather was a gentle man of great kindness and understanding, and he said that the person who had taken our battery probably did so only because he was too poor to buy one. Therefore, Hank said, he would not place a curse on the thief that would strike him instantly dead but merely one that would make all his skin fall off. Suddenly. All at once. While he was square dancing Saturday night. And just as he was winking at the prettiest girl at the dance. As we trudged along the dusty road, Hank kept adding to and improving upon the curse until it seemed to me that the kinder thing would be to have the thief struck instantly dead.

Presently a car came by headed in the direction of town, and we waved it down. The driver was an elderly lady with a little flowered hat on her head. She asked if we would like a ride, and we said yes, but there seemed to be a problem. The lady had two large dogs in the car with her, and they were carrying on as if we were the first decent meal they had seen in months. Hank suggested that maybe he and I could just stand on the running boards, one of us on each side, and that way, "heh, heh," we wouldn't disturb her dogs. The lady said that would be just fine. "Hold on good and tight," she warned.

We immediately discovered that she had not offered this bit of advice frivolously. She took off so fast our fishing lines came loose and cracked like whips in the air behind us. We were a quarter-mile down the road before our hats hit the ground back at the starting point, not that either Hank or I were concerned with such minor details at the moment.

The lady seemed to think she needed to explain the sudden start. She rolled down her window and shouted out, "Bad clutch!"

Hank arched what he called his "vitals" back from the snapping jaws of a dog. "All right!" he yelled. "Perfectly all right!"

As the lady rolled the window back up, Hank and I dug our fingernails deeper into the rain gutters on the roof of the car and clutched our fishing rods with our armpits. By then we were traveling sufficiently fast that grasshoppers were splattering on our clothes. And still the car seemed to pick up speed. Again the driver rolled down her window and the dogs competed with each other to see which would be first to get a bite of Hank's belly.

"Bad gas pedal!" she shouted out, by way of explaining the speed with which we were hurtling down the road.

"All right! All right!" Hank cried.

She rolled the window back up.

A grasshopper exploded on the left lens of my spectacles. The air was being sucked from my lungs. My fingers were paralyzed, and I wasn't sure how much longer I could hang on. Then the situation took a sharp turn for the worse. A deputy sheriff's car sped by in the opposite direction. Upon seeing us about to break the world's record for fastest ride on running boards, the deputy whipped a bootlegger's turn in the road and came roaring up behind us with red light flashing and siren going. Hank released one hand and pounded on the glass to get the little old lady's attention. When she looked at him, he pointed back at the deputy sheriff. She smiled and nodded and pushed the faulty accelerator pedal to the floor. The deputy stayed right on our rear bumper. Every so often he would try to pass, but the old lady would cut over in front of him and force him to drop back. Then the driver rolled down her window again and grinned up at Hank. "What'd you think of that? Pretty fancy bit of driving for an old lady, huh?"

"All right! All right!" Hank said, as one of the dogs clipped a button off the front of his pants.

"Wait till you see the way I handle my rod!" she yelled, cackling wildly as she rolled the window up.

"What'd she say?" I yelled at Hank.

"She said, 'Wait till you see the way I handle my rod!'" Hank screamed back at me over the roof of the car.

"That's what I thought she said. What do you make of it?"

"I think she's going to shoot it out with the *bleeping* deputy," Hank screeched.

"I thought that's what you'd make of it," I yelled back. "She must be some kind of criminal!"

"Yeah, the crazy kind!"

At that instant the old lady whipped the car over to

the edge of the road and braked to a stop in a cloud of dust. Hank and I dropped from the running boards, coughing and gasping, and wiped our eyes with our deformed fingers. The deputy slid to a stop on the opposite side of the road, and both he and the old lady jumped out of their cars and went into gunfighter crouches, the deputy's hand hovering over the butt of his revolver.

"Oh my gosh!" Hank moaned.

Then the dogs went for the deputy. Both of them leaped simultaneously for what I thought would be the jugular, but he caught them both in his arms and staggered backwards as they licked his face and wagged their tails.

"Heeeee heeeee!" the deputy laughed.

"Heeeee heeeee!" echoed the old lady. Then she pointed at the deputy and said, "That there's my son, Rod! Ain't he somethin'? I can still handle the big bugger, though!"

"Caught you again, Ma!" the deputy squealed.

"Only 'cause I had to be careful these fellas didn't fall off the running boards, that's the only reason!" Ma shouted back.

"Somebody stole my battery," Hank said to the deputy.

"You don't say," the deputy said. "Well, I got to be going. Lots of crime in these here parts. Y'all be careful now, ya hear?" And he took off in pursuit of crime.

The old lady ordered the dogs back into the car, and they obeyed instantly, scarcely bothering to take a snap or two at Hank.

"Well, hop back on the running boards and hold on good and tight," she said to us, "and I'll haul you fellas on into town."

"Thanks anyway," Hank said, "but we can walk from

here. Can't be much more than five miles to the nearest town."

"Fifteen," the old lady said.

"Shucks, is that all?" Hank said. "Why that's even better than I figured. Thanks again for the lift."

That's the sort of comment that not only saves the outdoorsman embarrassment but enables him to survive.

Journal of
An Expedition

☞ ☞ ☞ **R**ummaging through my files some time
ago, I happened across the journal I kept as leader of the
expedition to Tuttle Lake during the winter of '75. I was
immediately struck by the similarity the record of that
momentous and heroic struggle bore to the journals of
earlier explorers of the North American continent, and,
lest it be lost to posterity, I immediately began editing the
material for publication.

The other members of the expeditionary force
consisted of my next-door neighbor, Al Finley, and my
lifelong friend, Retch Sweeney. Neither man was particularly enthusiastic when I first broached the idea of a
mid-winter excursion to Tuttle Lake.

"You must be crazy!" Finley said. "Why would we
want to do a stupid thing like that?"

"Well, certainly not for fame or fortune," I said.
"We'd do it for the simple reason that Tuttle Lake is
there."

"Hunh?" Retch said. "Ain't it there in the summer?"

"Of course it's there in the summer," I told him

irritably. "What I mean is that it would be challenge for the sake of challenge."

Finley pointed out that there were two feet of snow on the ground.

"We'll use snowshoes," I told him. "We'll start early Saturday morning, snowshoe into Tuttle Lake, spend the night in my mountain tent, and snowshoe back out Sunday. It'll be a blast."

"Gee, I don't know," Finley said. "I've never been on snowshoes before. I better not go."

"That's a wise decision, Finley," Retch said. "A man your age shouldn't take any more chances than he has to."

"What kind of snowshoes should I buy?" Finley said.

Thus it was that the three of us found ourselves at trail's head, preparing for the assault on Tuttle Lake. The journal of the expedition begins at that point.

History of the Tuttle Lake Expedition
Under the Command of Patrick F. McManus

JANUARY 18, 1975—9:22 A.M. The weather being fair and pleasant, the men are in high spirits as they unload our provisions and baggage from the wagon for the trek into the mountains. The drivers of the wagon, a Mrs. Finley and a Mrs. Sweeney, offered to wager two of the men that they would "freeze off" various parts of their anatomy. I warned the men against gambling, particularly with wagon drivers, who are a singularly rough and untrustworthy lot. The throttle-skinners hurled a few parting jibes in our direction and drove away, leaving behind a billowing cloud of snow. This cloud apparently concealed from their view the man Retch Sweeney, who raced down the road after the departing wagon, shouting "Stop, Ethel, stop! I left the fifth of Old Thumbsucker

under the front seat!" It was truly a heartrending
spectacle.

9:45 A.M. I have assumed command of the expeditionary force. The men informed me that this is a false
assumption, but I will not tolerate insubordination,
particularly at such an early stage in the journey. I
threatened both of them with suspension of rations from
my hip flask. They immediately acquiesced to the old
military principle that he who has remembered his hip
flask gets to command.

11:00 A.M. The expedition has suffered an unexpect-
ed delay. I had directed two of the men to take turns
carrying the Snappy-Up mountain tent, but it made them
top-heavy and kept toppling them into the snow. We have
now solved the difficulty by obtaining an old toboggan
from a friendly native, who seemed delighted over the
handful of trifles he requested for it. On future expeditions I must remember to bring more of those little green
papers engraved with the portrait of President Jackson,
for the natives seem fond of them.

All of our provisions and baggage are lashed to the
toboggan, and I have directed the men to take turns
pulling it. I myself remain burdened with the heavy
weight of command. Rations from the hip flask cheered
the men much and, for the time being, have defused
their impulse to mutiny.

12:05 P.M. We have been on the trail for an hour.
Our slow progress is a cause of some concern, since by
now I had expected to be out of sight of our staging area.
Part of the delay is due to Mr. Finley, who is voicing a
complaint common to those who travel for the first time
on snowshoes. He says he is experiencing shooting pains
at the points where his legs hook on to the rest of him. To
use his phrase, he feels like "the wishbone of a turkey on
the day after Thanksgiving." I counseled him to keep

tramping along and that eventually the pains would fade away. For the sake of his morale, I did not elaborate on my use of the term "eventually," by which I meant "in approximately three weeks."

1:10 P.M. We have stopped for lunch. Tempers are growing short. After kindling the propane camp stove, I had to settle a dispute between the men about who got to roast a wiener first. I narrowly was able to avert a brawl when Mr. Sweeney bumped a tree and dumped snow from a branch into Mr. Finley's Cup-a-Soup. Mr. Sweeney claims the mishap was unintentional, but his manner of bursting out in loud giggles gives me some cause for doubt. I have had to quick-draw the hip flask several times in order to preserve order.

I sent one of the men ahead to scout for a sign to Tuttle Lake. He returned shortly to the main party, very much excited, and reported a large number of fresh tracks. I went out with him to examine the tracks and to determine whether they were those of hostiles. Upon close study of the imprint of treads in the tracks, I concluded that a band of Sno-Putts had passed through earlier in the day. Upon our return to camp, the band of Sno-Putts appeared in the distance, and, sighting our party, came near and gunned their engines at us. After the exchange of a few friendly taunts, they went on their way.

For the last half-mile, Mr. Finley has been snowshoeing in a manner that suggests he is straddling an invisible barrel. We attempt to distract him from his discomfort with copious ridicule.

We are now about to begin the last leg of our journey—a two-mile ascent of Tuttle Mountain. The weather has turned raw and bitter.

5:05 P.M. After a lengthy and difficult climb, we have at last arrived at our destination—Tuttle Lake. During our ascent of the mountain, I found it prudent to order frequent rest stops, since I feared the excessive wheezing of the men might bring avalanches down upon us. Indeed, such was the extreme state of my own weariness that I at first did not grasp the obvious fact that we had arrived at Tuttle Lake. Mr. Finley was the first to make the discovery.

"This is Tuttle Lake," he gasped.

"I don't see no lake," Mr. Sweeney said.

"This is Tuttle Lake!" Mr. Finley shouted. "We make camp here!"

It took but a moment for me to perceive that Mr. Finley was correct in his assessment of the situation; the lake is frozen over and blanketed with a good three feet of snow. We are no doubt standing above its very surface. I am filled with wonderment, not only that we have finally triumphed in achieving the noble purpose of the expedition, but that Tuttle Lake should cling at an angle of forty-five degrees to the side of a mountain.

Snow is now falling with an intensity that beggars the imagination; either that, or we are caught in an avalanche. We are unable to see more than a yard before our faces. It is imperative that we get the Snappy-Up tent erected immediately.

7:15 P.M. The [obscenity deleted] Snappy-Up tent is not yet up. We are taking a rest break, whilst Mr. Sweeney, employing a cigarette lighter, attempts to thaw his handlebar mustache, which he fears might snap off if bumped. Mr. Finley went behind the tent to bury a snow anchor, whereupon he discovered a precipice. The drop was not great, or so we judged from the brief duration of his scream. The rest of the party were about to divide his share from the hip flask when they detected sounds of someone or something ascending the slope. We assumed it to be Mr. Finley, since few men and even fewer wild beasts possess the ability to curse in three languages. We celebrated his return with double rations from the hip flask.

9:30 P.M. We are now ensconced in our sleeping bags in the tent, after devouring a hearty stew, which I myself prepared. Darkness and the considerable violence of the snowstorm prevented me from reading the labels on the packages of dried food, which I emptied into the cooking pot. I then supplemented these basic victuals with a can of pork 'n' beans, several handfuls of spaghetti, four boiled eggs, six onions, half a head of cabbage, six wieners, a package of sliced salami, one wool mitten (recovered from the pot after dinner), and a sprig of parsley. The men were full of compliments about the tasty meal, although not until after I served dessert —each a cupful from the hip flask.

Strangely, I have been unable to find my package of pipe tobacco, which I had stashed in the provisions sack for safekeeping. It seems to have been replaced by a package of freeze-dried shrimp curry. Since smoking shrimp curry may be injurious to one's health, I have denied myself the pleasure of an after-dinner pipe. The disappearance of the tobacco is a matter of no little curiosity to me.

Upon preparing to enter his sleeping bag, which is of the style known as "mummy," Mr. Finley discovered that the snowshoeing had bowed his legs to such an exaggerated degree that he was unable to thrust them into the bag. The alternative of freezing to death or allowing Mr. Sweeney and me to straighten his legs was put to Mr. Finley. He pondered the alternative for some time and finally decided upon the latter course. I administered to him from the hip flask a portion commonly referred to as a "stiff belt," and, whilst Mr. Finley clamped his teeth on a rolled-up pair of spare socks, Mr. Sweeney and I bent his legs back into a rough approximation of their original attitude and inserted Mr. Finley into his bag, he now being capable only of drunken babbling. Now, to sleep.

JANUARY 19, 1975—1:30 A.M. Have just been startled awake by a ghastly growling seeming to originate from just outside the tent. After failing to frighten off the creature by the subterfuge of breathing rapidly, I regrouped my senses and immediately determined that the growling was gastronomical in nature and was emanating from the expeditionary force itself. I was suffering from a monumental case of indigestion, an affliction that comes upon me every time I succumb to eating parsley. My men, who seemingly possessed no greater immunity to that treacherous herb than I, moaned dreadfully in their sleep. In the knowledge that the growling is caused by something we've eaten rather than something we might be eaten by, I shall once again retreat into deep but fitful slumber.

6:15 A.M. The day dawned clear and cold. The men arose early, kindled the propane camp stove, and huddled around it for warmth. I have no notion of the temperature but have deduced from the fact that frost keeps forming on the flames that it is considerably below the freezing mark. The men complain bitterly over the loss to the cold of various parts of their anatomy, and I could not help but remind them of my advice pertaining to betting the wagon drivers against that possibility. They failed to express any gratitude, choosing instead to make threats on my life.

It is becoming increasingly clear to me that the hardships encountered on this expedition have taken a great toll on the men. They both say they have no appetite for breakfast and claim to have a strong taste of tobacco in their mouths, even though neither has been smoking. This sort of delusion is common among members of expeditions, and it is only with a great act of will that I force myself to the realization that the bits of pipe tobacco stuck in my teeth are only imaginary. When I try to encourage the men to down a few bites of frozen shrimp curry, they can only shudder and make strange gagging sounds that are scarcely audible over the chattering of their teeth. I realize now that time is of the essence, and that we must prepare for the return journey with the greatest expedience. The men realize this also, and without waiting for the command, rip the Snappy-Up tent from its icy moorings, wrap it around the baggage and leftover provisions, and heave the whole of it onto the toboggan.

I dispense to each man a generous ration from the hip flask. The retreat from Tuttle Lake begins.

7:35 A.M. We have descended the mountain much sooner than expected and, indeed, much faster than the main body of the party deemed either possible or agreeable. In the event that I fail to survive this expedition and so that the offending party may be suitably disciplined, I offer this account of the affair: Upon realizing that my hip flask was either empty or contained not more than a single shot which would not be wasted on him, Mr. Finley mutinied. He refused to take his turn at pulling the toboggan. He sat down in the snow alongside the craft and displayed a countenance that can only be described as pouting. After arguing with him briefly, Mr. Sweeney and I went off down the mountain without him. It was our mutual judgment that Mr. Finley would pursue and catch up with us, as soon as he came to his senses. We had progressed scarcely two nundred yards down from the campsite when we heard a fiendish shout ring out from above us. Upon turning, we could hardly believe what we saw, and it was a fraction of a second before we realized the full import of the mutinous madman's folly. He was perched atop the mound of baggage on the toboggan and hurtling down the slope toward us at a frightful speed. Before we could external-ize the oaths forming on our tongues, he had descended close enough for us to make out quite clearly that he was grinning maniacally. "How do you steer one of these things?" he shouted at us. Dispensing with any attempt at reply, the main party broke into a spirited sprint that would have been considered respectable for Olympic athletes even if it had not been executed on snowshoes. All was for naught. The flying toboggan caught us in mid-stride, flipped us in the air, and added us to its already sizable load. We descended to the foot of the mountain in this unsightly fashion, clipping off saplings, blasting through snowdrifts, and touching down only on the high places. The ride, in retrospect, was quite exhilarating, but I was unable to overcome my apprehen-sion for what awaited us at its termination. This appre-hension turned out to be entirely justified. Indeed, some of the finer fragments of the toboggan are still floating down out of the air like so much confetti. Immediately upon regaining consciousness, Mr. Sweeney and I took up clubs and pursued the unremorseful villain across the icy wastes, but the spectacle of Mr. Finley plunging frantically through the snow, even as he laughed insane-ly, struck us as so pathetic that we were unable to administer to him the punishment he so justly deserved.

12:30 P.M. The wagon drivers rendezvoused with us at the appointed time, and we are now luxuriating in the warmth of the wagon's heater. The mutineer Finley has been pardoned, perhaps too soon, since he has taken to bragging monotonously of his exploits on the expedition to Tuttle Lake.

"I wouldn't mind doing that again," he said "How about you fellows?"

"Perhaps," I replied, "but only for fame and fortune. I've had enough of just-because-it's-there."

"I'll tell you one thing," Mr. Sweeney said to me. "The next time I go on one of these winter expeditions, I'm going to get me a hip flask just like yours. Where do you buy that two-quart size, anyway?"

Before I entrust him with that information, I shall have to assure myself he is fit for command.